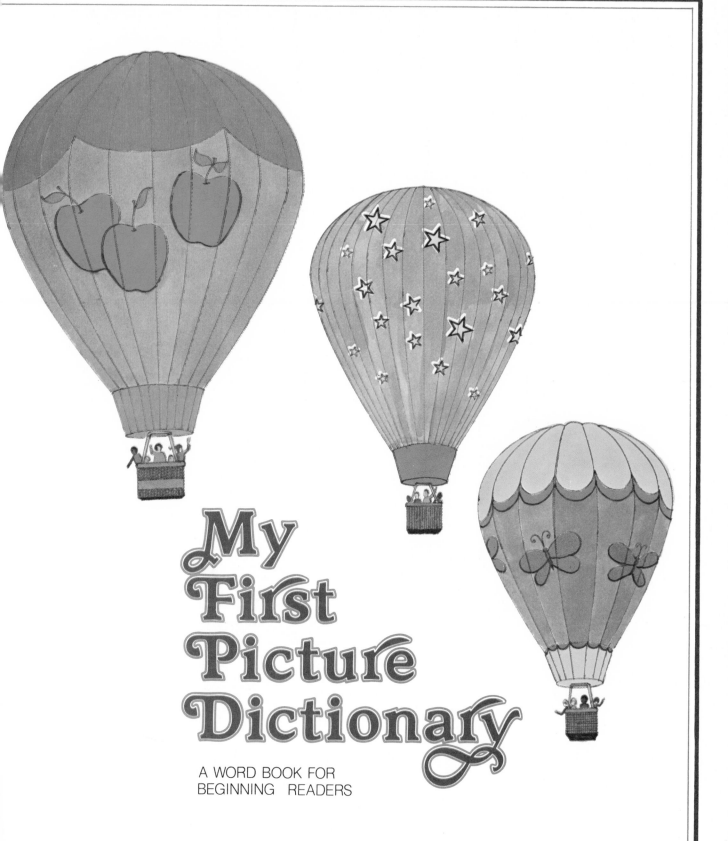

My First Picture Dictionary

A WORD BOOK FOR
BEGINNING READERS

My First Picture Dictionary

A WORD BOOK FOR BEGINNING READERS

Written and Designed by Kathleen Harshberger
Illustrated by Beverly and Richard Johnston

DERRYDALE BOOKS
New York

Copyright © 1982 by OBC, Inc.

All rights reserved.

This 1986 edition is published by Derrydale Books, distributed by Crown Publishers, Inc., 225 Park Avenue South, New York, New York 10003

Manufactured in Belgium

Library of Congress Cataloging in Publication Data

Harshberger, Kathleen.
    My first picture dictionary.

    Summary: Defines more than 1100 vocabulary entries and uses some 500 illustrations.
    1. Picture dictionaries, English. [1. English language—Dictionaries] I. Johnston, Beverly, ill. II. Johnston, Richard, ill. III. Title.
PE1629.H28 1986   423'.1   86-6226
ISBN 0-517-44379-1

h g f e d c b a

SOME NOTES FOR PARENTS ABOUT THIS BOOK...

Dictionaries, of all kinds, are tools to be used to expand and improve use of language. Your child by now probably knows the alphabet—the "ABCs"—and is moving fast in his or her grasp of language skills—reading, writing, spelling. Your child has an understanding of a certain number of words, written and spoken. Your child almost certainly uses a large number of words automatically, and correctly, in everyday speech and is now starting to organize and to master the use of those words in the written form. It is time for a first dictionary to help the beginning reader make the jump to mastery of the words he or she already uses in day-to-day speech and to stimulate that new reader to achieve mastery in more subtle vocabulary areas. That is the purpose of this book.

With more than eleven hundred entry words that combine very basic words already well established in the child's language (such as *a, able, about, above*) and vocabulary-expanding words (such as *accident, adult, ache*), the early reader is moved from one level of language ability to the next. Familiar words are defined, or put into context in sentences using clear, basic language. The reader will be encouraged to think about the words, individually, and in combination with other words. As a series of letters are organized in a certain way to form a word so, too, the reader will be guided to grasp the meaning of a word and then to think about it in relationship with other words to express a clear thought.

Since children are attracted, stimulated, and interested by color and illustrations, we have used full-color illustrations to engage the reader and to reinforce the learning that is in progress. We have chosen to illustrate certain words. The criteria for using an illustration has been that the illustration provide the best possible way to make the meaning of the word absolutely clear to the reader. The illustrations, when used, stimulate readers to look at the drawing, think about the word and, eventually, understand and use the word in written and spoken language.

Parents may find it best, in the beginning, to sit with the child and look at the book—page by page—reading and discussing what is seen and read. At that time, a parent may wish to look at the dividers that begin each section and play a guessing game with the child to see if he or she can name the objects on the page. You may wish to explain that the dictionary puts words in alphabetical order and try to help the child understand what that means. You and your new reader will find other word games come to mind as you go through the book together.

Learning, at best, is a lifelong adventure. Learning skill in language is an exciting process and a critical one. We hope, with this book, to help your child make a smooth transition from the "ABCs" to a real grasp, an understanding, of his or her vocabulary and to make it possible for the new reader to begin to acquire the learning in many areas that will come only after language skills are developed.

the Editor

Have fun with your book.

Look it over.

Note that the words are listed **Alphabetically.** All the words beginning with **A** are together, all the words beginning with the letter **B** are together, etc. **A** words come before **B** words, **B** words come before **C** words, and so on.

Look at the pictures.

Point out the things you know.

Take a look at the names of those things.

Close your eyes and try to see the word.

Think about how you would spell the word.

ictionary

OR, use the book to help find out what a word means. For example, let's find out what the word **hose** means.

Step 1. You may have seen the word **hose** and you think you know how it is spelled—or at least you have some idea how it might be spelled and know for sure it begins with the letter **h.**

Step 2. Since all the words in this book are in order according to the alphabet, you would go to the part of the book with words beginning with the letter **h.** The **h** section begins on page 80.

Step 3. Next, you have to find the second letter in **hose** from the list of **h** words. You then go through the words starting with ha - he - hi and finally come to page 87, where you find **honk** at the top of the page. Then you look at the third letter in the word **hose.** Ho **s** e comes after ho **r** n and so you find **hose.** You also find:

1. The word **hose** has two meanings. So you read both and decide which meaning you wish to use.
2. You will notice that if there is more than one **hose** being written or spoken about, the plural word is spelled **hoses.**
3. There is a picture of one kind of **hose.** You might want to think what a picture of the other kind of **hose** would look like.

So you have found your word and now you know a lot about it.

Let's go on to the next word.

Can you name the things on this page that begin with the letter A? See answers at bottom of page.

ABCDEFGHIJKLM
NOPQRSTUVWXYZ

and

1. I put peanut butter on the bread with some jelly. I made a peanut butter **and** jelly sandwich.
2. Five **and** five are ten.

angry

My little sister wrinkled my homework paper. She made me mad. I was **angry** with her.

another

Maureen had a little brother. Then she got **another** brother. Now she has two brothers.

answer

Answer means reply.

"Would you like lunch now?" asked his mother. "Yes, please," he replied. That was his **answer.**

any

1. I like **any** kind of candy.
2. Do we have **any** milk left?

April

April is the fourth month of the year. **April** has 30 days. It comes between March and May.

area

Area means a particular place.

1. The playground is the children's **area**. It is where children play.
2. Places where there are mountains and snow are often called ski **areas**.

(play) area

army

An **army** is a group of people who act together for a special reason. Most countries have an **army** of soldiers who would fight, if there was a war, to protect the people in that country.

around

1. We went **around** the block on our bicycles. We circled the block many times.
2. We stayed **around** the neighborhood all day.

arrive

To **arrive** means to reach a place. We **arrive** home after school. Mom and Dad **arrive** at their offices in the morning.

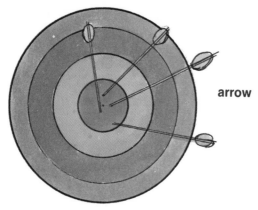

arrow

ARCHERY RANGE

arrow

1. Arrows have long, thin shafts that look like sticks with points at one end and feathers at the other end. **Arrows** are used with bows for shooting.
2. An **arrow** is sometimes used to show a direction.

art

Art is a kind of learning. It is a way of doing something. Painting, music, sculpture are **arts** but the study of medicine or engineering might also be an **art**.

ash

1. Ash is the name of a special kind of tree.
2. Ash is what is left when the fire goes out. There are **ashes** in the fireplace when the logs are burned.

ashamed

Sometimes, when we do something bad, we feel **ashamed**. If I hit my sister, I would feel badly about it; I would be **ashamed** of myself.

asleep

Asleep means to be sleeping. I am usually **asleep** by nine o'clock.

at

1. Dad was **at** the wheel of the car. He was driving. **2.** I get up **at** seven o'clock. **3.** We met **at** Stephen's house for lunch.

attention

The coach tells us how to hold the ball the right way. He has our **attention**. We listen carefully and pay close **attention.**

asleep

awake

August

August is the eighth month of the year. There are thirty-one days in the month of **August**. It is between July and September.

author

An **author** is someone who writes something. When you think of a story and write it down, you are the **author** of that story.

Autumn

Autumn is one of the four seasons. It is also called the Fall of the year. It is after Summer and before Winter.

awake

When you stop sleeping, you are **awake**. On school days, we **awaken** at seven o'clock. Sometimes I am **awake** before that.

Autumn leaves

away

Away means absent or gone.

If you give your toys **away**, you don't have them any longer. When we go **away** on vacation, we are gone from our homes.

Can you name the things on this page that begin with the letter B? See answers at bottom of page.

ABCDEFGHIJKLMN
OPQRSTUVWXYZ

bake
When you **bake** an apple, you put it in a heated oven to cook. The heat causes the apple to get soft and juicy. **Baking** is one way to cook food.

ball
Balls are round and can be rolled. They are sometimes made of rubber, or plastic or leather. **Balls** are an important part of many games such as baseball, basketball, golf, and soccer.

balloon
A **balloon** is a bag made of rubber, or cloth, that is filled with a gas or heated air so that it will float.

band
A **band** is a group of musicians who play their instruments together. Marching **bands** play music in parades.

barber
A **barber** cuts hair. **Barbers** use scissors and combs to cut hair neatly.

bare
When something is without its usual covering, we say it is **bare**. In the summer when you do not wear shoes, you are **bare**foot. In winter, when the leaves have fallen, the trees are **bare**.

bark
1. **Bark** is the outside covering on trees. **Bark** is usually brown, hard and rough to the touch.
2. The loud noise that dogs make is called **barking**.

barrel
A **barrel** is a round, hollow container that holds things. In some grocery stores, you can find a wooden **barrel** with pickles in it.

hot air **balloon**

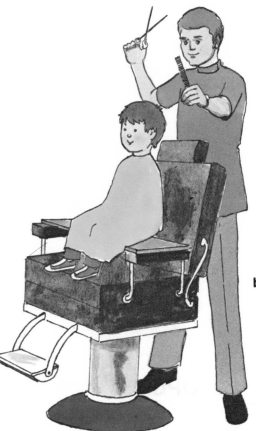

barber

17

base

1. The **base** is the bottom part on certain things that helps them stay in an upright position. The bottom part of lamps, beneath the part that holds the bulb, is called the lamp **base.**

2. The **bases** used in baseball are sand-filled bags. The players touch first, second, third, and home **bases** after they hit the ball.

base

basket

A **basket** is made of wicker, is sometimes shaped like a bowl and is used to hold things such as vegetables, fruit or flowers.

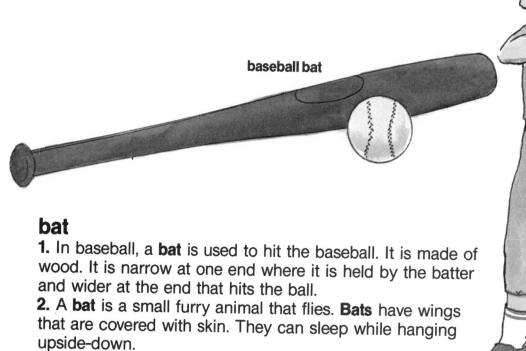

baseball bat

bat

1. In baseball, a **bat** is used to hit the baseball. It is made of wood. It is narrow at one end where it is held by the batter and wider at the end that hits the ball.

2. A **bat** is a small furry animal that flies. **Bats** have wings that are covered with skin. They can sleep while hanging upside-down.

be

Be is a verb. Some forms of **be** are: am, is, are, was, were, being, been.

1. Let's **be** good!

2. I am going to **be** home at three o'clock today.

beach

The **beach** is the sandy area along the seashore.

beak

Birds have **beaks**. The **beak** is the hard, pointy part of the bird's mouth.

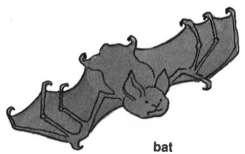

bat

beat

1. When you win a game, you **beat** the other team because your score is better
than theirs.
2. To scramble eggs, you **beat** the eggs with a fork or an eggbeater.
3. You **beat** the drum with drumsticks.

beautiful

Beautiful means very pretty or very good.

because

We couldn't go out today **because** it was raining. The reason we couldn't go out was that we would have gotten wet.

become

Little kittens grow up and **become** big cats. Puppies **become** dogs.

The girl is behind the tree.

before

1. Before we can go out, we have to eat breakfast. After breakfast we can go.
2. We never played this game **before**. This is the first time we are playing it.

behave

If you do the things your Mom and Dad tell you to do, they will say you **behave** nicely. If not, you will be **behaving** badly.

behind

Behind means in back of something.

The little mouse ran **behind** the chair. Now he is **behind** the clock and we can't see him.

believe

Believe means thinking, feeling or being convinced of something. I **believe** that Santa Claus lives at the North Pole.

below

Below means under or the opposite of above.

My brother and I have bunk beds. His is on the bottom; mine is on the top. His bed is **below** mine.

bend

When you **bend** something you force its shape to change.

When you exercise you **bend** your body so that your fingers can touch your toes.

bend

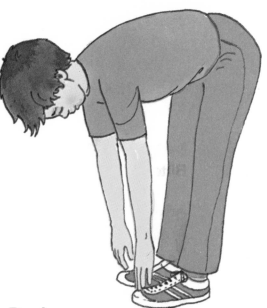

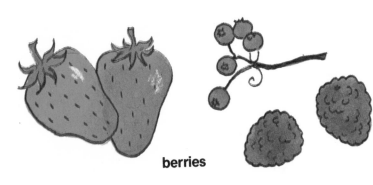

berries

berry

A **berry** is a fruit that usually grows on a bush. **Berries** are small and juicy.

bill

beside

Beside means next to.

At school, each desk is **beside** another one.

between

1. A hamburger has meat **between** two pieces of bread.
2. I like both the red dress and the blue one. I can't choose **between** them.

bill

1. A **bill** is a charge for goods or services. When you go to the dentist, you receive a **bill** for the work done by the dentist.
2. A **bill** is a kind of beak that some birds have.

bit

1. A **bit** is a small amount, a piece. I'd like a little **bit** of that cake.
2. Bit is part of the verb **bite**. When I **bit** into that cookie, I broke a tooth.

blacksmith

bitter

Bitter means ugly or sour tasting. Lemons taste **bitter**.

blacksmith

A **blacksmith** is a person that works with iron to make tools, shoes for horses and other iron things.

blanket

A **blanket** is a flat cloth made of wool or cotton or other fiber that is used, usually on beds, to keep people warm while sleeping.

blanket

blew

Blew is part of the verb **blow**. At my party, I **blew** out all the candles on the cake.

blind

Blind means not being able to see. My grandfather had an accident and his eye was badly hurt. Now he is **blind** in one eye.

block

Block means to stop.

When a beaver builds a dam in a stream, it **blocks** the flow of water in the stream.

blood

Blood is the red liquid in our bodies that carries things we need to live from one part of the body to another.

blew

blossom

A **blossom** is the flower of a fruit tree. **Blossoms** appear on certain trees in the Spring.

blossom

blow

1. On your birthday, you **blow** out the candles on your cake.

2. When the wind is **blowing** sailboats are able to move on the water because the wind fills the sails.

board

A **board** is a flat piece of wood that has been cut to a certain size and thickness. To build a treehouse, you need lots of **boards**, nails, a hammer and, of course, a tree.

boil

When water is heated to a certain hotness, it will **boil**. When water **boils**, it bubbles and gives off steam.

border

1. There are **borders** between countries so that everyone will know where one country ends and another begins.

2. A **border** is the edge around something. This page has a red **border**.

born

If today is your fifth birthday, it means you were **born** five years ago on this date. That was the first day there was a you living and breathing on your own and separate from your Mom's body.

both

I have a cat and a dog. They are **both** my pets.

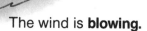

The wind is **blowing.**

bottle

A **bottle** is made to hold a liquid. **Bottles** may be plastic, glass or any material that will keep the liquid from passing through it. **Bottles** are usually round with flat bottoms and narrow tops.

bottom

The **bottom** is the lowest part. My pencil is at the **bottom** of my schoolbag.

bow

1. A **bow** is a kind of knot tied into a rope or cord to keep something closed. **Bows** are put on presents.

2. In archery, a **bow** is a long curved piece of wood with ends pulled together by a piece of cord or other material.

bow

bowl

Bowls are used to hold food while it is being prepared for cooking or to eat from. **Bowls** are round with high sides and deep centers. They are made of many materials such as pottery, glass and plastic.

box

A **box** is a five or six-sided structure of paper, wood or other material. **Boxes** hold things. Do you have a toybox?

brain

The **brain** is the part of our bodies that makes it possible for us to think and to give directions to the rest of the body. The **brain** is in the head.

box

brave

If you do something even though it scares you, you are being **brave.** The first time you ride a two-wheeled bicycle, you are indeed very **brave.**

break

1. If a glass drops onto the floor, it will probably **break** into many pieces.

2. If you cross the street when the traffic light is red, not green, you are **breaking** the law. You have done something wrong.

breakfast

breakfast

Breakfast is the meal you eat in the morning. It is the first meal of the day. A good **breakfast** might be fruit juice, cereal and milk.

breath

Breath is the air that enters our bodies through the mouth or nose in order that we can breathe.

breathe

When you **breathe**, you take air into your body by inhaling it and force air out of the body by exhaling it. When you run, you **breathe** hard.

brick

A **brick** is a piece of clay, shaped like a rectangle, that is baked so that it is very hard. **Bricks** are used for building houses.

bright

1. On a **bright**, sunny day, there are no clouds and the sun seems to light everything up.

2. **Bright** means shiny, sparkling.

bring

Bring means to take something or someone someplace. After school, children **bring** their books home.

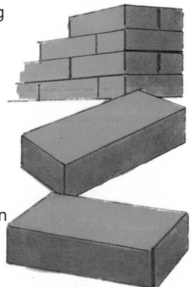

bricks

broke

Broke is part of the verb **break**. I **broke** my pen today. I would not have **broken** it if I hadn't pressed so hard on the point.

brother

If there is more than one child in a family, the boys are **brothers** to the other children (the girls are sisters).

brought

Brought is part of the verb **bring**. I **brought** my books to school today.

bubble

Bubbles are round, like balls, and have air inside them. Soap **bubbles** are so light that they float in the air.

Can you make **bubbles** with **bubble** gum?

bucket

A **bucket** is used to hold and carry things such as water or sand. **Buckets** are round with flat bottoms. They are deep and have handles for carrying them. They may be made of wood, or metal or plastic.

build

When you put layer on top of layer of sand in a certain way, you **build** a sand castle. Wooden blocks are used to **build** playhouses.

bucket

bull

Bulls are male cattle. Cattle are large animals that are raised on farms or ranches. They eat grass or hay and are raised mostly for food for people to eat.

bull

bulldozer

A **bulldozer** is a very large machine that can be driven like a car. **Bulldozers** are used to move earth around by using the large metal scoopers they have attached to them.

bump

A **bump** is a slightly raised and rounded spot. I have a **bump** on my head in the place where I hit my head on the door.

burn

1. If fire touches paper, the paper will start to **burn**. There will be flames and the paper will turn to ash.

2. The sun was hot yesterday. I stayed on the beach too long and the sun **burned** my skin. The **sunburn** was hot and it hurt.

busy

Busy means having many things to do.

but

1. I like baseball, **but** I like football better.
2. I like all sports **but** one. I like all sports except football.

butter

Butter is a soft, pale yellow food that is made from the cream part of cow's milk. It is whipped until it gets thick enough to be spread. **Butter** is good on bread and it can be used for cooking.

button

A **button** is a round, plastic, metal or wooden disc with small holes in it so that it can be attached with thread to cloth. **Buttons** and **buttonholes** make it possible to open and close clothing.

button

buy

When we exchange money for something we want, we **buy** it. If I had an allowance, I could **buy** candy.

by

1. Erin made dinner. Dinner was cooked **by** Erin.
2. She should be ready **by** now. She is always ready at this time.

buzz

buzz

Buzz is a sound made by a **doorbuzzer** or, perhaps, by bumblebees.

A child is pressing the **doorbuzzer.**

Can you name the things on this page that begin with the letter C? See answers at bottom of page.

ABCDEFGHIJKLMN
OPQRSTUVWXYZ

caboose
The **caboose** is the last car on a railroad train.

caboose

cactus
Cactus is a plant that grows in a dry, hot place such as a desert.

cake

cake
Cake is a sweet, bread-like food. **Cakes** are made of flour, sugar, eggs and milk. They are baked in the oven and eaten as dessert.

calf
A **calf** is a young cow or the young of certain other animals, as the elephant, seal and whale.

calf

call
1. I need a coin to make a telephone **call** to my parents.
2. I'll **call** you when dinner is ready. Stay near home so you can hear me **calling** you.
3. Have you given your puppy a name? What will you **call** him?

calm
Calm means still, without motion.

When the sea is **calm**, there isn't enough wind to make sailboats move and so they are still in the water.

came
Came is part of the verb **come**. Will you **come** to my party this year? You **came** last year.

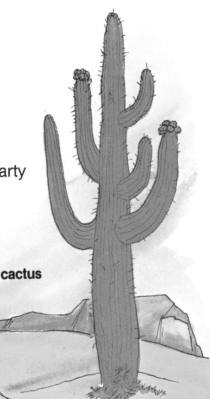

cactus

camel

Camels are large animals that are used for travel in the desert because they don't need much water. **Camels** can have one or two humps on their backs.

camera

A **camera** is a small machine that takes photographs. A special material called film is used in **cameras** to record the picture.

can

1. I learned arithmetic in school. Now I **can** add and subtract numbers.
2. Mom will allow me to go out after dinner but I **can** only stay out for an hour.

camel

candle

Candles are made of wax in a long, thin shape. There are pieces of wick, or cord, that run down the middle of the **candle**. When the wick is lighted with a match, the **candle** burns and gives off light.

cannot

We **cannot** watch television tonight but we can play games.

cap

1. A **cap** is a small hat such as a baseball **cap**.
2. A **cap** is the top or seal put on a bottle or jar.

car

A **car** is an automobile. **Cars** have engines, wheels and a place for passengers to sit. **Cars** travel on roads and highways.

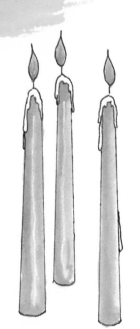

candles

care

1. I take **care** of my puppy. I feed him, walk him and play with him.
2. I don't **care** if it rains; I have lots of things to do indoors.

careful

If you are **careful** with your puppy, you try to make sure that no harm comes to him. You don't let him run into the street where he could be hurt.

carry

When I go to school I **carry** my books in a bookbag. I **carry** my lunch in a lunchbox.

cartoon

A **cartoon** is a picture that shows people and things in a special and funny way. **Cartoons** are drawn by artists.

catch

Catch means to grab or capture something. The **catcher** in baseball **catches** the ball as it comes across home plate.

caterpillar

A **caterpillar** is the wormlike larva of a butterfly or moth. **Caterpillars** are soft and furry. **Caterpillars** change into butterflies or moths.

cattle

Cattle are animals such as cows, bulls or steers that are raised by people for the food they provide.

carry

caterpillar

caught

Caught is part of the verb **catch**.

The first baseman **caught** the ball that the batter hit.

caught

cause

Ice is slippery. If you walk on it and fall, you can say the slippery ice is the **cause** of your fall.

cave

A **cave** is a hollow area in the earth . In ancient times, people lived in **caves.**

ceiling

The **ceiling** is part of the the inner lining of a room that is overhead. Most ceilings are about eight feet above the floor.

cellar

The **cellar** is the room or space that is under a house. **Cellars** sometimes have a furnace in them or they may be used to store things.

cent

cent

A **cent** is a very small amount of money. Pennies are coins that are worth one **cent**. One dollar is equal to one hundred **cents.**

center

The **center** means the middle or the mid-point. To get two equal pieces of cake, you cut the whole cake right across the **center.**

cereal

Cereal is the grain from a plant. Some **cereal** grains are wheat, rice and barley. **Cereal** is good to eat at breakfast.

chance

1. It looks stormy outside but I'll take a **chance** that it won't rain and go fishing.
2. It is my **chance** at bat. It's my turn to hit the ball.

change

1. This morning the sun was shining; now it is raining. That was a big **change** in the weather.
2. After school, do you **change** from school clothes to play clothes?
3. Mom gave me a dollar. I spent twenty cents so I have eighty cents **change** left from the dollar.

chase

Chase means to pursue, to go after. When you play tennis, sometimes you have to **chase** the ball to hit it.

check

1. Mom writes a **check** to pay for our rent. A **check** is a piece of paper that can be used to pass money from one person to another.
2. **Checks** are shapes with four sides of equal size. There are red and black **checks** on checker boards. **Checks** are used as designs on many things around the house such as cloth, pottery and rugs.
3. Dad comes into my room every night to **check** to make sure I'm sleeping.

cheek

The **cheeks** are part of the face. The **cheeks** are under the eyes and above the jawbone. In cold weather, the **cheeks** get rosy.

cheer

1. When I am happy, I feel full of good **cheer**.
2. At football games, sometimes there are **cheerleaders** who do **cheers** when the team does well.

cheerleaders cheering

cheese
Cheese is a food that is made from the milk of cows or goats.

chew
Chewing means crushing or grinding with the teeth. When you take a bite of an apple, you **chew** it and then swallow it.

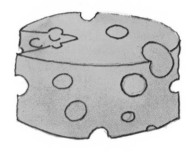

cheese

chief
The **chief** is the leader, the person in charge. The fire **chief** tells the firefighters how he wants them to go about their job.

chimney
The **chimney** is part of a house or building. The **chimney** carries smoke from a fireplace or furnace away from the house or building.

chimney

chin
The **chin** is the lowest part of the face. It is below the mouth.

chocolate
Chocolate is a food made from cocoa seeds mixed with sugar. **Chocolate** is brown in color and is eaten as candy or used as a flavoring when cooking things such as **chocolate** cake, **chocolate** pudding, etc.

chocolate

choose
To **choose** means to select from a number of things. I could have had an apple, a banana or a pear. I **chose** the apple. Which would you **choose?**

circle

1. A **circle** is a round shape such as a ring or a wheel.
2. At storytime, all the children form a **circle** around the teacher and she reads to us.

class

A **class** is a number of people, often in school, who are learning the same things at the same time.

My **class** learned ten new words today at school.

claws

claw

A **claw** is the sharp, hooked nail of a bird or other animal.

Cats use their **claws** to grab onto tree bark so they can climb trees.

clay

Clay is a soft mud-like material found in the earth that can be formed into bricks or pottery.

clean

1. When we wash our hands with soap and water, the dirt is washed away. Then our hands are **clean.**
2. On Saturday, I **clean** my room. I dust and sweep it and put away all the messy things.

clear

1. When the weather is **clear**, not cloudy or foggy, we can see great distances. If it is a **clear** night, we can even see the stars.
2. After dinner it is my job to **clear** the table. I take all the dishes and put them in the kitchen sink.

clever

My little brother is very **clever**. He figured out a way to get my candy from the top shelf in my room by putting chairs and toys on top of each other so he could climb up and reach the shelf.

climb

Climb means to go upward or downward using arms and legs. Don't you like to **climb** to the highest branch in an apple tree?

close

1. **Close** means near. Please sit **close** to me so we can talk.
2. **Close** means to shut. I **close** the door when I leave home.

closet

Closets are very small areas in houses that are used as a place to keep clothing and other things such as fishing poles, baseball mitts, etc.

cloth

When wool, cotton or other fiber is woven, it becomes **cloth. Cloth** is needed to make clothing and many things that are used in the home.

cocoon

The **cocoon** is the covering that caterpillars weave for themselves to live in until they turn into butterflies.

coin

A **coin** is a round, flat piece of metal that is used for money. Pennies, nickels, dimes, and quarters are **coins.**

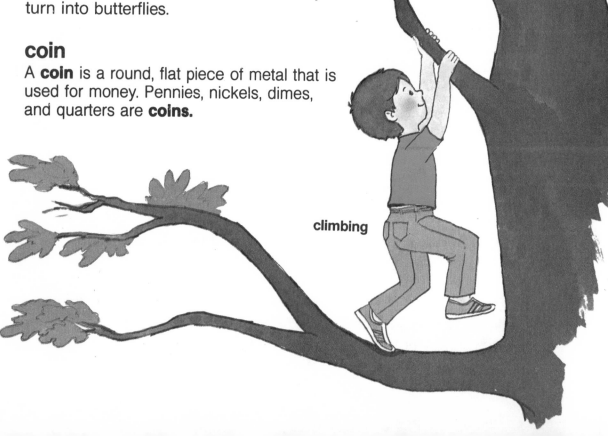

climbing

cold

1. Ice is **cold**; fire is hot.
2. If you sneeze, cough, have a stuffed nose and just feel badly you probably have a **cold**. A **cold** is an illness that makes people feel sick but does not last very long and is not usually too serious.

collect

Collect means to gather together. At the seashore you can walk along and **collect** many different kinds of shells. You can put together a shell collection.

comb

A **comb** is a tool used to separate strands of the hair and keep hair from getting knotted. **Combs** are usually made of plastic, rubber or metal.

come

1. Christmas **comes** once a year, on December 25.
2. Will you **come** over to my house?
3. My favorite pickles **come** in a funny glass jar.

A collection of combs

complain

My brother won't let me play with his cars. I **complained** to Mom and Dad that he is being mean to me. They told me not to **complain** so much.

complete

1. In order to **complete** the crossword puzzle, you must fill in all the boxes.
2. This is the **complete** set of encyclopedia. There are no books missing.

cone

Cones have round openings at one end and are twisted to closed points at the other end. Ice cream scoops are put into **cones.**

cones

confuse

Identical twins **confuse** their friends. People can't always tell which twin is which.

consonant

In the English alphabet there are two kinds of letters—vowels and **consonants. Consonants** are the letters B, C, D, F, G, H, J, K, L, M, N, P, Q, R, S, T, V, W, X, Y, and Z.

continue

I hope you will **continue** doing your work until it is finished.

control

If you want a dog, you must be able to **control** it and make sure it doesn't get loose on neighbors' property.

cook

1. Cook means to change food from its raw state by heating it. Pizza dough, tomato, cheese, and oil **cook** nicely together to make pizza pie.

2. A **cook** is a person who **cooks** the pizza or any other food.

cookie

A **cookie** is a small, flat, round, sweet, baked cake.

copper

Copper is a metal that is used to make certain coins, some kinds of pipes, special pots for cooking and many other things.

copy

1. The art teacher drew a clown on the blackboard. She asked us to try to make a **copy** of her drawing in our books. We tried to make our clowns look just like hers.

2. I borrowed this book from the library. There were two other **copies** of the same book left on the bookshelves.

cook

corner

The **corner** is the place where two sides meet. There are sometimes traffic lights and street signs on street **corners.**

correct

Correct means to set right or to be right.

1. After an exam, the teacher collects the papers to **correct** them. She checks to see if all the answers are right.

2. When the traffic light is green, it is the **correct** time to cross the street.

cost

We pay ten cents for chewing gum. The gum **costs** ten cents. The **cost** of the gum is ten cents.

costume

A **costume** is clothing worn when you want to pretend you are a different person or from a different place or time. At Halloween, children wear **costumes** that are scary.

cotton

Cotton is the soft, white fiber of the **cotton** plant. **Cotton** is woven into cloth that is used to make clothing and things for the home.

could

Could is a form of the verb **can.**

When I was young, I **could** run five blocks. Now I **can** run twenty blocks.

count

Will you **count** the apples in the basket? Then we will know how many apples we have. I think there are about twenty apples.

costumes

cover

1. A hat is a **cover** for your head. It protects your head from cold and rain.
2. To keep soup from splattering all over the place, we **cover** the pot with a lid.

cowboy

A **cowboy** is a man who looks after cattle. **Cowboys** work on ranches.

crack

1. To make scrambled eggs, first you have to **crack** the egg shells and put the eggs in a bowl.
2. If you get a **crack** in the fishbowl, all the water will leak out.

crack

crash

We heard a loud, **crashing** noise. The sound was made when two cars ran into each other. No one was hurt in the **crash.**

crawl

Crawling is a way of moving. Babies **crawl** before they walk by pulling themselves along on their stomachs or on hands and knees.

crayon

A **crayon** is a pencil of colored wax that is used to write or draw.

cream

Cream is the thick, fatty part of milk that can be used for making butter or cheese. Soon after the milk is taken from the cow, the **cream** will rise to the top of the container and is then easily separated from the rest of the milk.

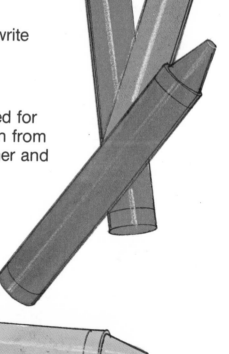

crayons

crocodile

A **crocodile** is a large, thick-skinned, lizard-like reptile. **Crocodiles** live in marshy areas in some tropical parts of the world.

crocodile

crooked

Crooked means bent, not straight. The picture on the wall is **crooked.** Someone should make it hang straight.

cross

1. This is the shape of a **cross.**

2. We **cross** the street to get to the other side.

3. Mom gets **cross** when we fight.

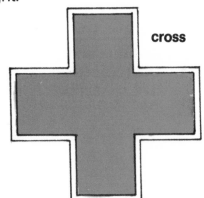

cross

crowd

A **crowd** is a number of people who are closely pressed together in a space. At parades there are **crowds** of people along the parade route.

crown

A **crown** is a special kind of covering for the head worn by a king or queen.

crown

cry

A **cry** is a sound made by a person who is upset for some reason. Babies **cry** if they are hungry or thirsty. Children and even adults **cry** if they are hurt or unhappy.

cup

Cups hold things such as milk or other liquids. They are round and may have handles on them so that they are easier to hold and to drink from. **Cups** are made of many things such as glass, metal, plastic, or wood.

cup

Cc

curious

Children are **curious** about many things. They want to know why the sky is blue, why the sun shines, where snow comes from and many other things. They want answers to questions.

curl

Curls are twisting spirals or curves. Some people have **curls** in their hair; some people have straight hair.

curve

A **curve** is a bending line. Highways **curve** as they go around mountains.

cut

To **cut** means to divide by using a sharp tool such as a knife or scissors. Mom **cuts** my sandwich into four pieces.

curls

curve

Can you name the things on this page that begin with the letter D? See answers at bottom of page.

ABCDEFGHIJKLMNOPQRSTUVWXYZ

Dad, Daddy

Dad or **Daddy** is the name some children call their fathers.

daisy

A **daisy** is a flower with white petals and a yellow center. Certain types of **daisies** have pink or yellow petals.

dam

A **dam** is a wall of earth or concrete built across a stream to hold back water.

damp

Damp means slightly wet or moist. After my hair is washed and partly dried with a towel, it stays **damp** for a long time.

dance

A **dance** is a special way of moving to the sound of music. You can **dance** using special steps as in ballet or you can make up your own **dance** steps.

dandelion

The **dandelion** is a flower that is bright yellow in color that grows wild in fields.

danger

A **danger** is something that may be harmful. There is **danger** in swimming too far out from shore. You may get tired or have a cramp and not be able to swim back.

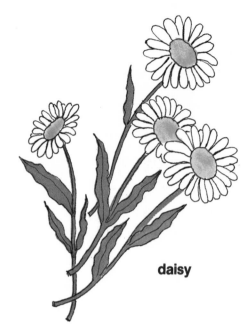

daisy

dance

dancer

dandelion

dark

At night it is **dark** outside. If you don't put on the lights in your house, it will be **dark** inside, too.

date

A **date** is a particular day. The **date** for Christmas is December 25. What is the **date** of your birthday?

day

1. The **day** starts at dawn and ends at sunset. The **day** is the time when the sun is out.
2. There are 24 hours in a **day**—from midnight to midnight. There are seven **days** in a week.

dead

Dead means not alive. If you don't water a plant, it will dry up and die. It will be **dead.**

dear

1. "**Dear** Suzy," the letter began. Most letters start with the greeting "**Dear.**"
2. She is my **dearest** friend. I love her more than anyone else.

December

December is the twelfth and last month of the year. Christmas is in **December.** There are thirty-one days in **December.**

decide

My friends want to play outside. I can't **decide** if I want to go out or stay at home. Finally, I **decide** to go.

day

date

December

deep

1. Out in the ocean the water is **deep**. It is far from the surface of the water to the ocean floor.
2. In the swimming pool, the water in the **deep** end is nine feet. In the shallow end it is two feet **deep**.

delicious

Delicious means to taste very good. That is the most **delicious** ice cream I have ever tasted.

describe

To **describe** is to tell everything you can about a person or thing. A **description** of something will give you a picture in your mind of that thing.

desert

A **desert** is a large area of land where there is almost no rainfall. The land is sandy and very little will grow there. **Deserts** are often hot during the day and cold at night.

design

When you **design** something, you decide how that thing should look and you do the work that will make it look the way you want. I **designed** a Christmas card for my parents. I made it with red and green paper. It had a picture of a pine tree on the cover and words inside. It was a pretty **design.**

dessert

dessert

The **dessert** is the last part of the meal. **Desserts** are usually sweet. Cake, ice cream, fruit, and pudding are all **desserts.**

diamond

1. Diamonds are very valuable jewels. They are mined from the earth in certain parts of the world. **Diamonds** are very hard and clear.

When cut carefully, they sparkle.
2. A **diamond** is a shape with four sides of equal length. A **diamond** shape is higher than it is wide.

diamond

dictionary

A **dictionary** is a book that tells the meaning of words. Words in a **dictionary** are put in alphabetical order to help find them quickly and easily.

did

Did is part of the verb **do.**
1. I must not tell a lie. I **did** chop down the cherry tree.
2. I **did** my homework when I got home today. I **do** it every day.

dictionary

die

When life goes out of something, it **dies.** After a few days, most flowers **die.** They dry up and fall off the plant. They are dead.

different

Different means not the same.

You are in the second grade. I am in the third grade. We are in **different** grades.

dig

Dig means to remove the top level to get at what ever is underneath. In the city when the electric company wants to fix the lines underneath the ground, they **dig** holes in the street.

dig

dime

A **dime** is an American coin that is worth ten cents. You need ten **dimes** to equal a dollar.

dip

dip

Dip means to put something into a liquid for a short time.
1. She **dipped** her spoon into the soup. Then she took it out and sipped the soup from the spoon.
2. I took a **dip** in the swimming pool. It was a very short swim.

direction

1. The four **directions** are north, south, east and west. Are we going in the right **direction?** We are supposed to be going north.

2. The **directions** on the package were to mix two eggs into the cake mix. That tells us how to make the cake.

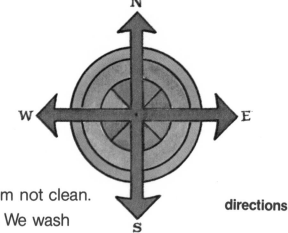

directions

dirt

Dirt is what gets into things that makes them not clean.

After playing in the mud, we get very **dirty**. We wash ourselves to get the **dirt** off.

disappear

When something **disappears**, you cannot see it.

Magicians seem to make things **disappear** and then reappear again.

distance

Distance is the amount of space from one object to another.

School is two blocks from my house. The **distance** from my house to school is two blocks.

dive

Dive means to plunge, head first, into water.

divide

Divide means to separate into parts.

Mom **divided** an apple into two parts for Jim and me.

dive

do

Do you ride your bike every day?

Did you ride yesterday?

Does your sister ride well?

doghouse

doghouse

A **doghouse** is a place, usually outdoors, for a dog to live. **Doghouses** look like tiny houses and are often in the backyard.

doll

A **doll** is a toy that looks like a baby or other human being.

dollar

A **dollar** is an amount of money. A **dollar** may be a single piece of specially printed paper or it can be one hundred pennies or ten dimes. A **dollar** is the same as one hundred cents.

done

Done is part of the verb **do.**

Have you **done** your homework? Will you **do** it now, please?

door

The **door** is the opening or passage into a room, house or other building.

doll

doughnut

A **doughnut** is a small round cake with a hole in the middle.

down

1. The ski lift will take you from the bottom of the mountain to the top. You will have to ski **down** the mountain.

2. Let's meet down at the bottom of the mountain.

3. Down is the fine soft feathers from birds, such as geese and ducks. Clothing made with **down** is very warm.

dozen

A **dozen** is a group of twelve of anything.

Eggs are usually sold by the **dozen.**

dragon

Dragons are creatures that we read about in fairy tales. They are imaginary animals that look like crocodiles with wings. They are scary because they have long claws and breathe fire.

drank

Drank is part of the verb **drink.**

Before he went to bed, he **drank** a glass of milk.

draw

1. Artists **draw** pictures of things using paper and crayons.
2. He pulled a ticket from the barrel. He **drew** the winning ticket.

dream

Dreaming is like thinking while you are asleep. When you **dream** you see pictures of people and things in your mind. Bad **dreams** are called nightmares.

dragon

50

dress

1. A **dress** is an article of clothing. **Dresses** are made of cloth and are usually worn by girls and women.
2. When you **dress** in the morning, you put your clothes on.

drew

Drew is part of the verb **draw.**

He **drew** in his breath and then quickly blew out the candles.

drink

1. Drink means to swallow water or other liquid. We **drink** from cups, glasses, bottles or even cans.

2. A cold **drink** of water is good when we are hot.

dress

drip

Drip means falling in drops.

That milk carton must have a hole in it. The milk is **dripping** onto the floor.

drive

A person **drives** when he causes a vehicle such as a car to start up and move along the road or highway.

When you are eighteen you can have a **driver's** license and **drive** your own car.

drive

driven

Driven is part of the verb **drive.**

The car was **driven** from New York to California.

drop

drop

1. Do not spill one **drop** of that water.
2. My little sister took the eggs out of the bag and **dropped** them on the floor. What a mess!

drove

Drove is part of the verb **drive.**

Last week we **drove** our car from New York to California.

drunk

Drunk is part of the verb **drink.**

My kitten is thirsty today. She has already **drunk** three plates of milk this morning.

dry

Dry means not wet.

It rained last night and there is water on the streets. We can't race on our bicycles until the streets are **dry** again.

digging

dug

Dug is part of the verb **dig.**

Yesterday we **dug** three holes in the yard and planted three new trees.

dull

1. The paint on the car used to be bright and shiny. Now it has become pale and **dull.**
2. The knife has become **dull.** It doesn't cut well anymore.
3. That television show is boring. I think I'll write and tell the station how **dull** it is.

dump

Dump means to throw down in a pile.

Please **dump** the garbage into that barrel.

dust

Dust is fine, dry pieces of earth.

After the wind storm there was **dust** all over my bicycle.

Can you name the things on this page that begin with the letter E? See answers at bottom of page.

ABCD**E**FGHIJKLMN
OPQRSTUVWXYZ

each

Each means every single one.

Each child in the class has his or her own books.

early

1. I woke up today before I usually do. I woke up **early.**
2. School starts at nine o'clock. I try to get there **early** so that I can play before school starts.

earth

1. Earth is the name of the planet we live on.

2. The soil that covers the dry portions of this planet is called **earth.** Plants and trees grow in the **earth.**

earth

earthquake

An **earthquake** is shaking or trembling of the ground. Sometimes **earthquakes** cause buildings to fall down.

east

East is a direction.

The sun rises in the **east.**

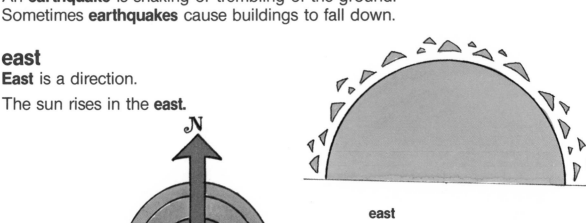

east

easy

Easy means free from difficulty.

I learned how to add three numbers. It was **easy** for me to learn that. Some things are harder to learn.

eat

When you put food into your mouth, chew it and then swallow it, you are **eating.** Everyone must **eat** in order to live.

eat

echo

If you are in a large, empty room and you shout, you may hear the sound you made twice. That is an **echo.**

edge

1. The cutting **edge** of a scissors or knife is the thin, sharp side.
2. We walked to the water's **edge.** That is where the water stops and dry land starts.

edge

either

Either means one or the other.

There are two cookies on the plate. You may have **either** one you wish.

else

Else means other, in addition.

I have started baking the cake. I would like someone **else** to finish it.

emerald

emeralds

An **emerald** is a green stone that is found in certain rocks.
Emeralds are cut and polished and used to make jewelry.

empty

The cookies are all gone. The cookie jar is **empty.**

end

1. When the story is over, that will be the **end** of the movie.
2. On one **end** of a pencil there is an eraser; on the other **end** is the lead point.

end

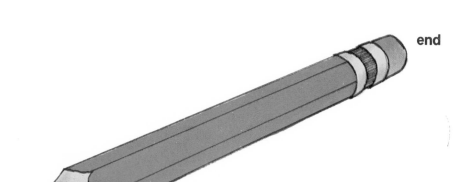

energy

Energy is the power that is needed to make things work.

Oil and coal are burned to give off the **energy** to make machines run. Food gives children the **energy** they need to grow.

engineer

1. An **engineer** is a person whose job it is to design and build things such as bridges, cars and buildings.
2. Engineers are also the people who run locomotives.

enjoy

To **enjoy** means to like or feel happy about something.

I **enjoy** going to the circus. I like the clowns and acrobats and elephants.

enough

We have ten candy apples and ten children. We will have **enough** candy apples for the children.

enter

Enter means to go in.

1. Most children **enter** Kindergarten when they are five years old.
2. We **entered** the playground by climbing over the fence.

engineer

entrance

An **entrance** is a doorway or passage into a place.

We pay for the tickets for the ball game at the **entrance** to the stadium.

Eskimo

Eskimos are a people who live in certain very cold parts of the United States and Canada.

Eskimo

especially

I like most of my teachers but I **especially** like my music teacher.
She is my favorite.

even

1. Even means flat or level. Before Mom painted the table, she
scraped the wood until it had a smooth, **even** surface.
2. Any number that can be divided by two without a remainder is
an **even** number. The numbers 2, 10, 50, 100 are all **even** numbers.
1, 3, 5, 7 are all odd numbers.
3. Even if you go, I am not going.
4. At the end of the game, the score was 50-50. The score
was **even.**

The score is **even.**

ever

Ever means at all or any times, always.

Did you **ever** hear the joke about the pink and green elephant?

every

Every means each one of the whole group. We want **every** piece of
candy that is in the box.

everybody, everyone

Everybody and **everyone** means every person. **Everybody** in my
class will be in school today. **Everyone** will be there.

everything

Everything means every object. **Everything** in the desk belongs
to me.

everywhere

Everywhere means in every place. I looked **everywhere** for the doll
I lost.

evil

Evil is something that is very bad or that causes pain.

In the story of Snow White, the **evil** witch gave Snow White a poisoned apple.

excellent

Excellent means very, very good. You did a very fine drawing of that tree. That was an **excellent** drawing.

except

There were five girls in the gymnastics class today. All **except** one used the balance beam. That girl had a sore leg.

exciting

Around Christmas time we think about Santa Claus and snow and toys. All that is very **exciting** to think about.

excuse

1. If you are sick, you will be **excused** from school. You won't have to go back until you are well again.
2. You must bring a written **excuse** from your parent when you return to school. The note will tell the reason that you were out.

exercise

1. In gym class, we stretch and bend and jump to **exercise** our bodies.

2. In spelling class we have workpapers called **exercises** to help us practice spelling.

exercise

exit

Exit is the name given to the door you go through to leave a room, building or vehicle.

In movie theaters there are red, lighted signs that say "**Exit**." They are at every doorway so that people will know how to get out of the theater in case of emergency.

expand

Expand means to spread out or unfold.

When you blow up a balloon, it **expands** until it is much larger than its starting size.

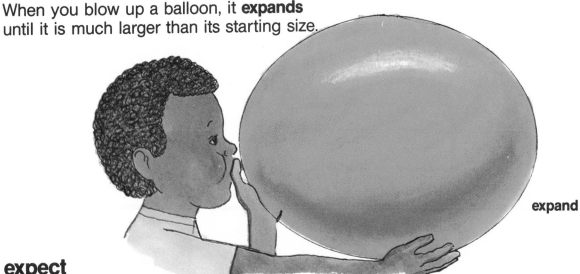

expand

expect

Grandmother is coming to our house today. We **expect** her to be here in time for lunch. We **expected** her earlier but she missed the train.

expensive

When the price of something is very high, that thing is **expensive.** It costs a lot of money.

explain

Explain means to make clear or plain. The teacher will **explain** about the planets and stars. She **explains** everything carefully so that we understand.

explode

If you put too much air into a balloon, it will **explode.** It will make a loud noise as the air escapes and it will break up into smaller pieces.

explode

explore

As soon as we got to our new house, we went out to **explore** the neighborhood. We found out where the stores and the playground and the school were. We **explored** until we learned all about the new town.

extra

We have six cupcakes and five children. If we give each child one cupcake, there will be one **extra** cupcake.

Can you name the things on this page that begin with the letter F? See answers at bottom of page.

ABCDE**F**GHIJKLMNOPQRSTUVWXYZ

fact

A **fact** is something that has really happened or is true.

It is a **fact** that snow is white, and soft, and cold.

fair

1. Mom makes me go to bed at 8 o'clock. My sister can stay up. I don't think that is **fair.**
2. The weather today will be **fair** and cool. It will not rain.
3. A **fair** is a place where people get together to show and sell things and to have fun.

fairy

A **fairy** is an imaginary person with magic powers.

In the story of Cinderella, her **fairy** godmother helps Cinderella.

fall

1. When you are learning to ride a bike, you have to be careful not to **fall** off the bike.
2. Fall is one of the four seasons. In the **Fall,** leaves turn pretty colors and then **fall** off the trees. Autumn is another name for the **Fall** season.

fan

When you are hot in the summer, you can turn on an electric **fan** that has flat blades that turn very quickly and cause the air to move and cool you off. If you make a **fan** from paper, you can cool yourself by waving it back and forth.

fancy

Fancy means not plain, special. Party clothes are often too **fancy** to wear to school.

far

Far means a great distance. I am allowed to go two blocks from my house. Your house is too **far** for me to go. It is three blocks away.

fairy

falling leaves

61

farther

I ran three miles today. I never ran that far before. That is **farther** than I've ever run.

fast

Fast means quick or speedy. Cats run very **fast.**

father

A **father** is a man who has a child.

father

favorite

Red is my **favorite** color. I like it more than any of the other colors.

fear

When I was little I used to be afraid of the dark. Now I don't **fear** the dark anymore.

feather

feather

A **feather** is part of the covering of a bird's body. **Feathers** are usually soft to the touch and are very light in weight.

February

February is the second month of the year. There are usually 28 days in **February** but in a Leap Year, **February** has 29 days. That happens every four years.

feathers

fee

A **fee** is what you pay for something that is done for you.

When you take a pet to the veterinarian, you will pay a **fee** or an amount of money so that the doctor will be paid for taking care of your pet.

feed

Feed means to give food.

I **feed** my dog every day before I go to school. I give him a can of dogfood.

feel

1. My kitten is sick. I **feel** very sad.
2. When I have a cold, I don't **feel** well.
3. I touched the gerbil's soft, fluffy fur. It **felt** nice.

female

A **female** is a girl or woman. **Female** is the sex that gives birth to young.

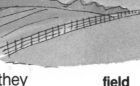

feed

few

Few means a small number.

There is hardly any candy left. There are only a **few** pieces in the box.

field

A **field** is a flat, open piece of land.

1. Airplanes land at **airfields.**
2. Vegetables and grains are grown in **fields** because they are flat and there are no trees to get in the way of planting.

field

fight

Little children **fight** with each other about toys or other things. They may push, or hit, or yell at each other. Each one wants to win the **fight** and to get or keep the toy.

fill

Mom asked me to **fill** the glass with milk. She wanted milk up to the top of the glass so the glass would be **full.**

find

1. I can't **find** my doll. She has been lost since yesterday.
2. I want to **find** out about the game. I don't know who won.

fine

1. I showed my teacher my drawing. She said I did a **fine** job on it. She thought it was very good.
2. I asked Dad if I could go with him to the store. He said, "**Fine**, let's go!"

finish

Finish means to bring to an end.

We start to eat dinner at about 6 o'clock and **finish** at 7 o'clock. When dinner is over, we go out to play.

fireplace

The **fireplace** is the lower part of a chimney that opens into a room. Wood is burned in the **fireplace. Fireplaces** are usually made of brick or stone and are used to warm the room.

fireworks

Fireworks are used at some celebrations. They are explosions of chemicals that give off bright, colorful lights and make loud noises.

fight

fireworks

first

Something that is **first** is before all others.

She was the **first** in her class to finish her work.

fist

A **fist** is a tightly closed hand.

Stephen used his **fist** to hit the punching bag.

fit

1. When my clothes get too small for me, they don't
fit anymore.
2. I was sick in bed for two days. The doctor said I will
be **fit** enough to go back to school by tomorrow.
I'll be well by then.

fix

Fix means to repair.

In order to **fix** my bike, I had to take the wheel off, get a
new tire, put it on, and put air in it.
Fixing the tire took all morning.

flame

Flames are part of a fire. They are red, yellow or blue.
They are very hot and are like long tongues of light that
move and flicker.

flames

flash

A **flash** is a sudden burst of light.

Lightning **flashes** in the sky. Sometime, if you are in a car
at night, you will see the headlights of other cars **flashing.**

flashlight

A **flashlight** is a small light that can be carried with you. It
needs batteries to work but will give light in the dark when
there are no other lamps around.

flashlight

flat

Flat means even or level.

The table is **flat.**

flavor

The **flavor** of something, usually food, is the way it tastes.

Do you like the **flavor** of vanilla ice cream better than the **flavor** of chocolate?

flew

Flew is part of the verb **fly.**

The airplane **flew** over our house today. Did you ever **fly** in an airplane?

float

Float means to rest on the surface of the water or other liquid.

Boats **float** in water.

flock

A **flock** is a group of animals of the same kind, especially sheep or birds.

flood

A **flood** is what happens when water rises and overflows the land. Heavy rains sometimes cause **floods** that destroy whole towns by washing away the houses.

floor

The **floor** is the part of the building that you walk on.

flock

flour

Flour is the fine powder that is made by grinding grain. **Flour** is used to make bread and cake.

flour

flown

Flown is part of the verb **fly.**

By the time the birds reached our city, they had **flown** hundreds of miles.

fly

1. A **fly** is a small insect with wings.
2. To **fly** means to move through the air on wings or by use of other kinds of power. Birds **fly** using their wings. Airplanes **fly** using the powerful engines and the wings of the plane.

fly

fog

Fog is a collection of many, many tiny droplets of water near the ground. It is very hard to see through **fog.**

fold

When you buy new clothes, they are usually **folded** neatly. Mom likes you to **fold** your clothing before you put anything away in the drawer.

Origami is the art of **folding** paper.

follow

1. My dog is always with me. He **follows** me everywhere I go.
2. I always read the rules that come with my games and I **follow** the rules carefully.

foot

1. The **foot** is the part of the body that is used to stand on and walk on. There are five toes on a person's **foot.**
2. A **foot** is a unit of measurement. There are twelve inches in a **foot.** A **foot** is the same as twelve inches.

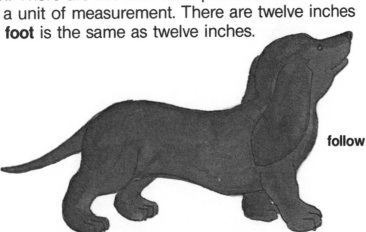

follow

for

1. Let's go **for** a walk.
2. This will be a word book **for** children.
3. The apples were two **for** a dollar. **For** one dollar, we were able to buy two apples.

forget

Forget means not to be able to remember.

If you don't write your assignment in a book, you may **forget** to do your work.

form

1. I will **form** the clay into the shape of an elephant.
2. Steam is one **form** of water. Ice is another **form** of water.

forward

Forward means toward the front.

The army sergeant said, "**Forward**, march!" The soldiers started marching straight across the field.

fought

Fought is part of the verb **fight**.

My kitten and puppy **fight** with each other. Yesterday, they **fought** in the living room and broke a lamp.

found

Found is part of the verb **find**.

I **found** my gloves in my pocket. Can you **find** yours?

fox

The **fox** is a wild animal of the dog family.

Foxes have long bushy

tails and are very alert.

fox

free

1. When you are not charged for something that you would usually pay for, that something is **free**. Did you ever get a **free** toy in a box of cereal?

2. Free means able to move about and do as one chooses. If a bird is in a cage, it cannot fly away so we say that it is not **free**.

freedom

Freedom means being free. If we let the bird out of its cage, we have given it **freedom**.

fresh

1. Vegetables and fruit that has just been picked is called **fresh**.

2. Water in the ocean is salty. The water in most lakes and rivers has no salt in it. That is called **fresh** water.

Friday

Friday is the sixth day of the week. **Friday** comes after **Thursday** and before **Saturday**.

friend

A **friend** is someone that you like very much and care about.

from

1. I taught my little brother to count **from** one to ten.

2. I ran all the way home **from** school.

front

The school bus picks us up in **front** of our house. We wait at the **front** door until the bus comes along.

friend

69

frost

When the weather gets very cold, the dew on the ground freezes and turns to **frost** which is very thin ice.

frown

If you are worried, confused or puzzled about something, you may squeeze your eyebrows together in a way that makes a funny face. That is called a **frown.**

fry

Fry means to cook in a pan using fat or oil.

full

Every seat on the school bus was taken. The bus was **full** of children.

funny

Funny means amusing. The clown we saw at the circus did **funny** things and wore **funny** clothes. He made us laugh.

fur

Fur is the hairy coating on the skin of certain animals.

future

The time that is to come is called the **future.**

Next year is the **future.** You will be an adult in the **future.**

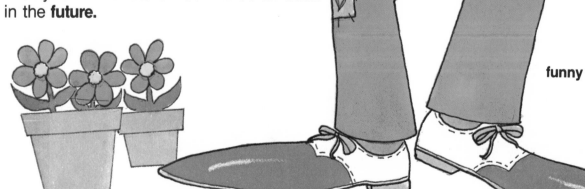

funny

Can you name the things on this page that begin with the letter G? See answers at bottom of page.

ABCDEFGHIJKLMNOPQRSTUVWXYZ

Gg

gallon
A **gallon** is an amount of liquid. There are four quarts in a **gallon.**

Some automobiles can be driven fifty miles using one **gallon** of gasoline.

gallon

garbage
Garbage is anything that is to be thrown away because it is broken, torn or in other ways used up.

After you have finished cutting up the paper dolls, put the paper scraps in the **garbage.**

gargle
When you **gargle** you put water or other liquid in your mouth, let it go deep into your throat and hold it there. Then you breathe slightly outward through the liquid to make bubbles and a **gargling** sound.

gate
A **gate** is a movable part of a fence that is the passageway in or out of a closed area.

gate

gather
Gather means to bring together, to collect.

Mom makes us **gather** our toys before we go to bed.

gave
Gave is part of the verb **give.**

She asked me to **give** her my telephone number. I **gave** it to her. She **had given** me her number already.

get
1. I **get** up in the morning at 7 o'clock.
2. I hope to **get** a new bike for my birthday.
3. I have to **get** to work on my homework.

gather

ghost

In stories, **ghosts** are spirits of dead persons that return to haunt the living.

giant

Giant means a person or thing that is larger than usual.

Jack climbed up a beanstalk and met a mean **giant.**

giddy

Giddy means jumpy, or dizzy.

Sometimes riding the roller coaster will make you feel **giddy.**

gigantic

Gigantic means very large, huge.

Elephants and whales are **gigantic** animals.

giggle

Giggle means to laugh in a silly way.

The girls started to **giggle** as soon as the teacher left the room.

ginger

Ginger is a spicy food that comes from the root of a plant.

Ginger ale and gingerbread are two foods we eat that have **ginger** flavoring.

gingerbread

Gingerbread is a sweet, spicy cake. It is light brown in color and has the taste of **ginger.**

giant

giraffe

A **giraffe** is an animal. **Giraffes** have long necks and can eat the leaves from the tops of trees.

girl

A **girl** is a young, female person. **Girls** grow up to be women.

give

Please **give** that pencil to me. I will **give** it back to you when I have finished using it.

glad

Glad means happy, merry, joyful.

Billy was **glad** when his friend came to play with him.

glare

Glare means to shine with a very bright light.

There was a **glare** from the snow when the sun was shining on it.

glass

1. Glass is a special material that has many uses because it is hard, transparent (you can see through it) and it can be molded into many shapes. Windows are made with **glass** so that light will come into rooms.

2. It is very healthy to drink eight **glasses** of water each day.

3. When people do not see well, they wear **eyeglasses** which are made of special **glass.**

glue

Glue is a thick, sticky liquid that is used to hold things together.

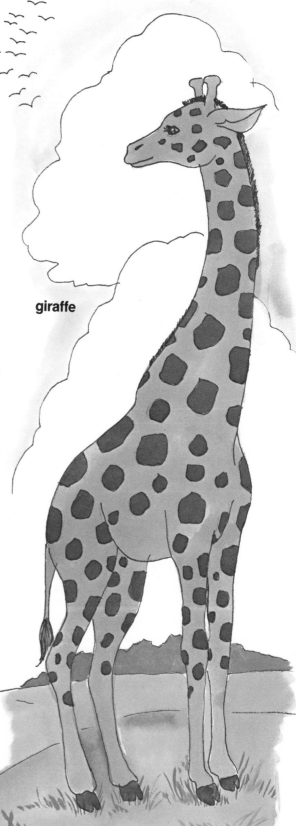

giraffe

go

Do you **go** to school by bus. I went by bus last year but now I **go** by car.

gold

Gold is a very valuable metal. **Gold** is a deep yellow color and is used to make jewelry and coins.

goldfish

Goldfish are small fish that are popular for home aquariums because of their color which ranges from yellow to orange.

goldfish

good

1. These are **good** boots for snowy weather. They are warm and dry.
2. They were **good** little puppies. They didn't misbehave all day.
3. This hamburger tastes very **good.**

good by, good-bye

When I leave home to go to school, I say "**Good by**," to my family.

goose

A **goose** is a web-footed bird. **Geese** are larger and have longer necks than ducks.

goose

got

Got is part of the verb **get.**

I **got** a good grade on my math test this week.

grade
After kindergarten children go into the first **grade.** Most schools have eight **grades.**

grain
1. A **grain** is a single seed or fruit of a food plant. Wheat, rye, oats and corn are **grains.**
2. The beach is made up of billions of **grains** of sand.

gram
A **gram** is a small amount of weight. One slice of white bread weighs about three **grams.**

grandparent
A **grandparent** is the parent of your parent. Your grandmother and grandfather are your **grandparents.**

grass
Grass is a green plant that is used as a food for some animals. **Grass** is also planted around buildings to make them look prettier.

grasshopper
A **grasshopper** is a leaping insect that lives in grass.

great
1. My teddy bear came in a **great** big box.
2. These cookies taste **great.** They are my favorite kind.

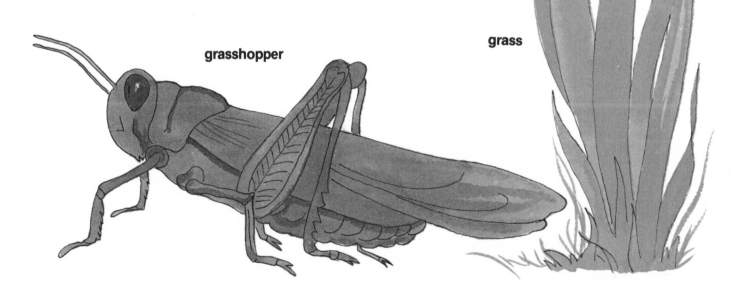

grass

grasshopper

green

Green is a color. Grass and trees and plants are **green.**
Green traffic lights mean it is all right to go across
the street.

grew

Grew is part of the verb **grow.**

In the Spring, red and yellow tulips **grew** in my yard. Now
roses are **growing** there.

grin

A **grin** is a very wide smile. Did you ever notice that cats
look as though they have **grins** on their faces?

grin

groceries

Groceries are foods and household items that we buy at
the supermarket.

ground

1. The **ground** is the surface of the earth, the land.
2. Meat is **ground** up into small pieces for hamburger.

group

A **group** is a number of persons or things that are together.
A **group** of children went swimming together.

grow

Apples **grow** on trees. After they are **grown** they are picked
for us to eat.

group

Gg

grownup

Grownup means not a child any more, a fully grown person, an adult.

guard

Guard means to protect or defend.

1. When money is delivered to the banks, there are special trucks and **guards** to be sure the money is not stolen.
2. I will **guard** your bike while you go into the store.

guess

Guess means to think or believe without being sure. I **guess** Mom will let us go to the movies.

gum

Gum is a soft, sticky substance. Chewing **gum** is fun.

grownup

Can you name the things on this page that begin with the letter H? See answers at bottom of page.

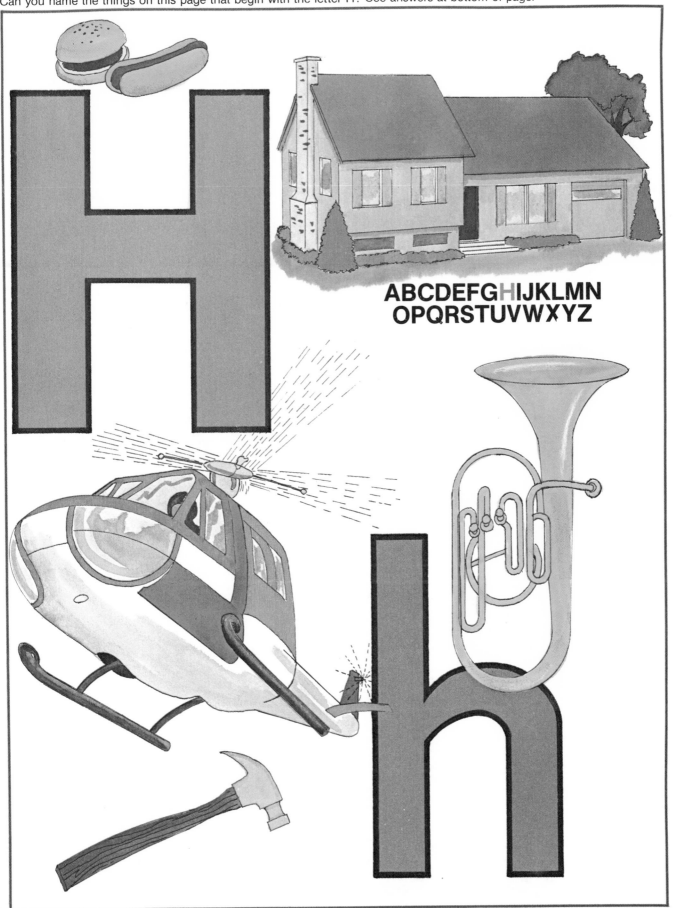

ABCDEFG**H**IJKLMN
OPQRSTUVWXYZ

habit

A **habit** is something you do over and over again, without thinking about it.

When I eat dinner, I always eat the meat first, then the vegetables, then the potatoes. That is my **habit.**

haircut

A **haircut** is the trimming, cutting or shaping of the hair.

half

A **half** is one of two equal parts. Mom cut the sandwich into two **halves.** I ate one **half.**

half

hall

A **hall** is a passageway connecting areas in a building.

hamburger

1. **Hamburger** is raw beef, chopped or ground up.
2. A **hamburger** is a sandwich of ground beef, broiled and placed in a round bun.

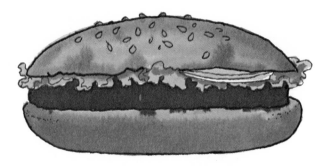

hamburger

hamster

A **hamster** is a small animal. It is a short-tailed rodent that burrows.

handkerchief

A **handkerchief** is a square piece of cotton, silk or linen cloth hemmed on all sides. **Handkerchiefs** can be used to cover your nose when you sneeze.

hamster

handle

1. Handles help us hold on to things. Pots have **handles** so they can be picked up safely and easily.
2. Puppies have to be **handled** very gently. When they are picked up, you have to be sure not to hurt them.

hang

At Christmastime, children **hang** ornaments on their Christmas tree. Each ornament has a little hook that can be attached so it will **hang** on the tree branch.

happen

What do you think will **happen** if you leave your bike out in the rain. It will get all rusty. That's what will **happen.**

hard

Hard means strong, solid, firm to the touch. Feel the difference between a **hard** baseball and a softball.

hardly

Hardly means barely, not quite. This shelf is very high. I can **hardly** reach it.

harmonica

A **harmonica** is a small musical instrument that has a small set of metal reeds in a little case. It is played by inhaling or exhaling breath across the reeds.

hang

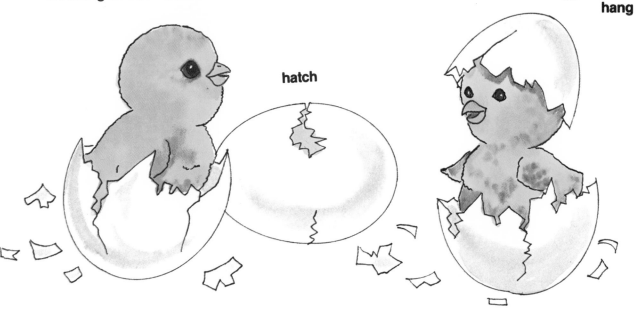

hatch

hatch

Chicks **hatch** when they peck themselves out of their eggs.

haunt

In stories, **haunted** houses have ghosts or spirits living in them.

have

Do you **have** any pets? I **have** one cat, two gerbils and eleven fish. I **had** fourteen fish but some died and I **haven't** replaced them.

he

He means the man or male. Dad is upstairs. **He** is sleeping. My dog is downstairs. **He** is eating.

heal

Heal means to make well and healthy again.

I broke the bone in my arm. It was put in a plaster cast and took six weeks to **heal.** Now it is good as new.

healthy

When we are not sick and feel good, we are **healthy.**

hear

We **hear** with our ears. We **hear** all the sounds around us, such as talking, traffic, barking of dogs, wind, and thunder.

heard

Heard is part of the verb **hear.**

I **heard** you singing in the shower. You sounded terrible!

haunt

heart

The **heart** is a part of the body. It is in the upper left side of the chest. The **heart** pumps the blood throughout the body.

heat

The furnace in your house makes the **heat** to keep you warm. Fire in the fireplace also helps to **heat** the house.

heavy

This suitcase has too much in it. It is too **heavy** for me to lift.

heel

1. The **heel** is the back, bottom part of the foot.
2. The **heel** is also part of the shoe that is under the back part of the foot. Little girls like wearing their mothers' high **heels.**

height

Height is a way of explaining how tall things are. The **height** of most rooms is eight feet from the floor to the ceiling.

held

Held is part of the verb **hold.**

1. Can you **hold** this candle for me? I **held** it for an hour.
2. The airplane **held** five hundred passengers. There were seats for that many people.

hello

Hello is a greeting. **Hello** is something you say when you meet people or answer the telephone.

heel

heel

help

Mom likes us to **help** make dinner. I peel potatoes and my brother sets the table. We also **help** by washing the dishes.

hen

A **hen** is a female chicken. **Hens** lay eggs.

her

1. This is Sally. I met **her** at the door.
2. This is my coat. That one is **her** coat.

here

Here means this particular place. **Here** is the pen. The pen is **here.**

hens

herself

My little sister is able to open the door **herself.**

hide

My dog likes to **hide** bones. He takes his bones into the yard, digs a hole and drops them in. They stay well **hidden** there.

high

1. The tree is thirty feet **high.** It is almost **higher** than the house.
2. He had a very **high** fever. He was very hot.

hill

A **hill** is a place on the earth where the ground is raised. A **hill** is much smaller than a mountain.

him

I saw Tommy up the street. I called out to **him.**

himself

He, **himself,** will do the work.

hippopotamus

A **hippopotamus** is a very large animal. It has a thick skin, a hairless body, short legs and a large head. It lives near the rivers and lakes of Africa. It can stay underwater for a long time.

his

This is **his** book. The book belongs to him.

hit

1. In baseball, batters **hit** the baseball with the bat.
2. The rock stars made a **hit** record.

hive

A **hive** is a place where bees live and work. Bees make honey in the **hive.**

hippopotamus

hill

hive

hobby

A **hobby** is something people do just for fun. Collecting things such as marbles or stamps is a **hobby.** Some people play golf or other sports as **hobbies.**

hockey

Hockey is a game that is played between two teams on ice using curved sticks and a small disc that is called a puck.

hockey

hole

A **hole** is an opening through anything.

1. Donuts have **holes** right in the middle of them.
2. I ran over a nail and put a **hole** in my bicycle tire.

hollow

Hollow is an empty space inside something. The chocolate Easter Bunny was **hollow.** It was not solid chocolate.

home

Your **home** is the place where you live.

honest

People who are **honest** tell the truth and never cheat or steal.

honey

Honey is the sweet, thick liquid that is made by bees. **Honey** is good to eat with bread.

honey

honk

Honk is a sound made by geese or a similar sound such as a car horn makes.

hook

A **hook** is a piece of curved metal that is used to catch or hold something. Fish are caught with **hooks.** Your coat can be hung on a **hook** in the hall.

hook

hop

A **hop** is a short little jump. Rabbits move by **hopping.**

hope

I **hope** to get good grades. That means I wish and want to get good marks.

horns

1. Horns grow on the heads of certain animals such as cattle, goats and deer.
2. Car **horns** make a noise to warn other drivers or people on the sidewalk.

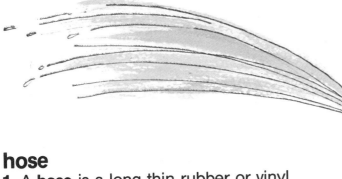

hose

hose

1. A **hose** is a long thin rubber or vinyl tube that is used to move water or some other liquid. **Hoses** are used to water the lawn.
2. Stockings and socks are also called **hose.**

hospital

A **hospital** is a place where people go if they are ill to receive care so they will get better. Doctors and nurses work in **hospitals.**

hot

Hot means very warm, fiery, peppery, heated. Fire is **hot.**

hot dog

A **hot dog** is food. **Hot dogs** are made from meat that is ground up and stuffed into a thin casing. **Hot dogs** are cooked and put on long rolls for eating.

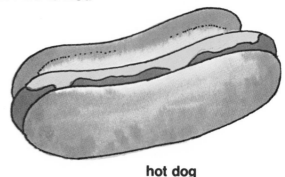

hot dog

how

1. **How** do you get to the library? Do you know the way?
2. **How** much does soda cost? What is the price of the soda?

however

1. I cannot go out today. **However,** tomorrow we can go to the movies.
2. **However** you can, please finish the story.

huge

Huge means very large. There is a **huge** stuffed teddy bear in my room. It is the biggest one I ever saw.

human

People are **human** beings. **Humanity** means all the people in the world.

hump

A **hump** is the large bump on the back of certain animals. Camels and bison have **humps.**

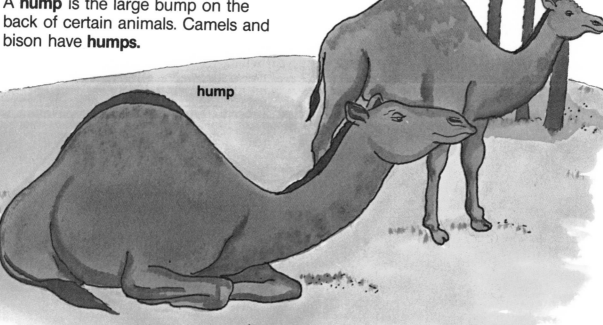

hump

hundred

A **hundred** is a collection of 100 of anything. The number one **hundred** is found between 99 and 101. There are ten tens in one **hundred.**

hung

Hung is part of the verb **hang.**

She **hung** her coat in the hall closet. It is full now so I will **hang** mine in here.

hungry

Hungry means feeling a need to eat.

When I get home from school, I am always **hungry** and so I eat fruit and milk.

hunt

Hunt means to search for or seek.

Have you ever been on a treasure **hunt**? All kinds of things are hidden and the players **hunt** until they find the treasures.

hurry

Hurry means to move faster. We have to **hurry** to be ready for the school bus in the morning.

hurt

1. I **hurt** my finger when I caught it in the door.
2. It **hurt** so much that I could not sleep.

husband

A **husband** is a man who agrees to share his life with a woman in marriage.

hurry

hut

Hut is a kind of home that is easy to build. Sometimes, kids build **huts** in their back yard and pretend they are castles.

hut

Can you name the things on this page that begin with the letter I? See answers at bottom of page.

ABCDEFGHIJKLMNOPQRSTUVWXYZ

ice

Ice is frozen water. When it gets cold enough for the lake to freeze over, it is hard enough to **ice** skate on.

iceberg

An **iceberg** is a very large piece of ice that has broken off from a glacier and has floated out to sea.

iceberg

ice skates

Ice skates are metal blades which may be attached to the bottom of leather boots or shoes. **Ice skates** make it possible to glide on ice.

icicle

An **icicle** is a long, thin, cone-shaped piece of ice formed by the freezing of water as it drips.

idea

An **idea** is a thought, a picture in your mind. When you wake up in the morning, you get **ideas** about what you will do that day.

if

1. You can watch some television **if** you finish your homework.

2. She asked **if** I thought we should go out.

3. If only it will snow, we can play all day.

ill

I ate too much cotton candy, and I felt **ill** all afternoon. My stomach ached.

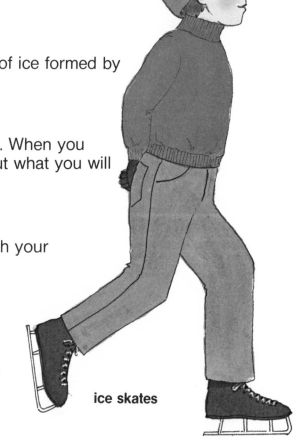

ice skates

I'll
I'll means I will. **I'll** be home at six o'clock.

I'm
I'm means I am. **I'm** going to the movies today.

imagine
Imagine means to form a picture in your mind about things that may not be real at present.

I **imagine** that when I grow up I will be an astronaut.

important
1. In order to do well at school it is **important** to do your homework. Homework helps you learn.
2. The leader of your country is a very **important** person.

impossible
Impossible means not able to be done. It is **impossible** to be in two places at one time.

in
1. We live **in** the city.
2. He can run a mile **in** five minutes.

inch
Inch is the name given to a small amount of length. There are twelve **inches** in one foot.

ink
Ink is a colored liquid used with pens for drawing and writing, or on printing presses for printing books, magazines, and newspapers.

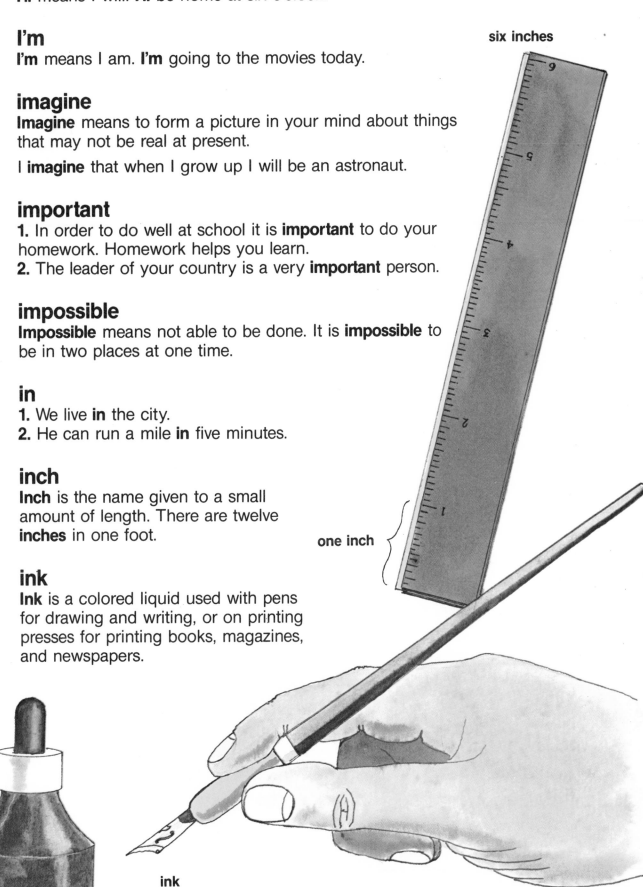

six inches

one inch

ink

inside

1. We are going **inside** the school building now.

2. There was a toy **inside** the cereal box.

instant

An **instant** is a very short amount of time, a moment.

1. The **instant** you arrive we will have lunch.
2. Come here this **instant!**

instead

Instead means in place of. I have a sandwich for lunch. I would like a hamburger **instead.**

instrument

1. Piano, drums and guitars are musical **instruments.**
2. Dentists use dental **instruments** to care for teeth.

interest

Erin tries to learn everything she can about horses. Horses are her **interest.** She is **interested** in horsey things.

into

1. He dived **into** the swimming pool.
2. We divided the pie **into** six equal pieces.

instruments

invent

Invent means to make something that no one has ever been able to make before. Eli Whitney **invented** the cotton gin to remove seeds from the cotton plant.

invention

The **invention** of the telephone made it possible to talk to people across distances. The telephone was an important **invention.**

invite

Invite means to ask a person to come to a place. I am going to **invite** ten children to my birthday party.

iron

1. **Iron** is a strong, hard metal.
2. An **iron** is a household appliance. It gets hot and is used to take wrinkles out of clothing.

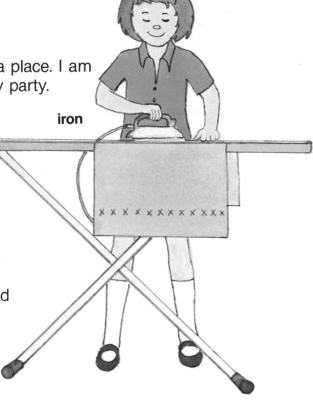

iron

is

Is is part of the verb **be.**

I **am** going to **be** seven this year. My friend **is** already seven.

island

An **island** is a piece of land with water all around it.

it

1. **It** is my fault. I broke the vase.
2. Who is **it? It's** Jeannie.

island

itch

I walked in some poison ivy and got a rash on my legs.
The rash **itches** me. I want to scratch the **itch.**

its

The dog went into **its** dog house.

it's

It's is a short way to write it is or it has. **It's** been two years
since we were to the circus.

itself

The cat squeezed **itself** through the pantry door.

ivy

Ivy is a very pretty plant. It has green leaves and climbs up
the sides of buildings.

ivy

Can you name the things on this page that begin with the letters J or K? See answers at bottom of page.

ABCDEFGHI JKLMN OPQRSTUVWXYZ

Jj

jail
A **jail** is a building where people must stay if they have broken the law.

jam
1. Mom gets angry when I **jam** my toys into the closet.
2. I love grape **jam.** It is made by cooking grapes and sugar together and tastes great on bread.

jam

January
January is the first month of the year. New Year's Day is on **January** 1st.

JANUARY					
1	2	3	4	5	6
7	8	9	10	11	12	13
14	15	16	17	18	20	21
22	23	24	25	26	27	28
29	30	31			

January

jar
Jars are made of glass, plastic or pottery and are used to hold things. Jam comes in a glass **jar** with a screw-on lid.

jaw
The **jaw** is one of two bones that forms the framework for the mouth.

jelly
Jelly is a soft, sweet food that is made with boiled fruit juice and sugar.

jewel
Stones such as diamonds, rubies and sapphires are **jewels.**

jewel

job.

A **job** is a piece of work.

My **job** is to set the table. Dad is a police officer. That is his **job.** Mom and Dad have **jobs** to earn money for our family.

jog

1. Jog means to push or shake slightly. The picture will **jog** your memory so you will be able to remember.
2. Jogging is a kind of slow running. People **jog** as exercise.

join

Join means to connect or bring together.

1. I want to **join** the tennis team next year.
2. Using glue, I was able to **join** the two pieces of wood.

joke

A **joke** is anything said or done to cause people to laugh. A **joke** can be a funny story or a riddle.

jolly

Jolly means gay, merry.

You are in a **jolly** mood today. You are laughing and joking and having a very good time.

joy

Joy is a sense of great happiness. When something very good happens to us or to our families or friends we feel **joy.**

juggle

Did you ever see anyone who could throw three or more balls into the air and keep them all there at the same time? That is a **juggler.** He or she **juggles** things to amuse people.

juggle

juggler

99

juice

Juice is the liquid part of fruits or vegetables. Fruit **juice** is made by squeezing the liquid out of the fruit.

July

July is the seventh month of the year. It has thirty one days and comes after June and before August.

jump

Jump means to lift your whole body so that you spring clear of the ground.

June

June is the sixth month of the year. June has thirty days and comes after May and before July.

jungle

A **jungle** is a kind of forest. **Jungles** are hot and wet. Certain plants and animals live in the jungle. Bananas, for example, grow well in **jungles.**

junk

Junk is a collection of old and broken things.

Mom says I have to get rid of all the **junk** that is in my room.

just

1. We say an umpire makes a **just** call when he decides what we think is fair to both teams.

2. That is **just** how I left them. Nothing has been changed.

jungle

keep

1. Once in a while, at school, the teacher has to remind us to **keep** quiet.

2. I've got five dollars. I'm going to **keep** two dollars so I can go to the movies and **keep** the other three dollars in a savings bank.

kept

Kept is a form of the verb **keep.**

I **kept** three dollars in the bank for two months.

ketchup

Ketchup is a good food. It is a thick mixture of tomatoes and spices and tastes very good on hamburgers.

ketchup

kettle

A **kettle** is a kind of pot usually used for boiling water. Some **kettles** whistle as the steam goes through the top.

key

keys

1. We need a **key** to open the lock. **Keys** are metal objects that fit into locks in such a way that when they are twisted the lock will open or close.

2. The **key** to the answer is in the first sentence. That **key** will help find the answer.

3. Pianos have **keys** that are struck to make the sound.

keyhole

The **keyhole** is the hole into which the key is inserted.

keyhole

kick

Kick means to strike with the foot.

My little brother likes to **kick** stones along the street all the way to school.

kill

Kill means to cause the death of something.

The frost came too early this year and **killed** the vegetables in my garden.

kilometer

A **kilometer** is an amount of distance. A **kilometer** is equal to 1,000 meters or .6214 miles.

kind

1. She is a very **kind** person. She cares a lot about people.

2. We can have oatmeal or wheat flakes for breakfast. Which **kind** of cereal do you want?

kindergarten

A **kindergarten** is a school for children who are usually about five years old. Children play and learn in **kindergarten.**

king

A **king** is a man who is the ruler of his country or tribe.

kingdom

A **kingdom** is a country where a king or queen rules.

kiss

A **kiss** is a gentle touching with the lips.

She picked up the kitten and **kissed** him on the head. Her brother didn't want to **kiss** the cat.

king

kit

A **kit** is a small case that holds things that are used for special purposes. For example, first aid **kits** contain things such as bandages and medicine to help if someone is hurt. Model **kits** contain all the things needed to build a model such as an airplane, boat, etc.

kite

A **kite** is a wooden or plastic frame covered with cloth or paper. **Kites** fly in the wind.

knew

Knew is part of the verb **know.**

He **knew** it was time to go home. He was wearing a watch and **knew** how to tell time.

knight

In medieval times, a **knight** was a man who was admitted to a military rank after serving as page and squire. **Knights** fought to defend the kingdom.

knock

1. There was a **knock** at the door. When I opened the door, I found it was Jimmy **knocking.**

2. When I played volleyball, I got **knocked** in the nose with the ball.

knot

I learned to tie my shoelaces when I was four years old. It was hard to learn to tie a **knot.**

know

1. I **know** the four times table by heart.
2. I **know** that I have to go to bed at nine o'clock.
3. My friend and I **have known** each other since kindergarten.

kites

knot

Can you name the things on this page that begin with the letter L? See answers at bottom of page.

ABCDEFGHIJKLMN
OPQRSTUVWXYZ

ladder

A **ladder** is a metal or wooden structure used to climb to a high place.

The painter used the **ladder** to reach the second floor of the house.

land

Land is the solid part of the earth's surface. People live on the **land.**

language

Language is a way people have to exchange thoughts and ideas.
Language is spoken or written. This book is written in the English language.

lap

When you sit down the upper part of your legs becomes your **lap.** Kittens and puppies like to sit on **laps.**

large

Large means having a big size.

Goldfish are small fish; sharks are **large** fish.

ladder

lasso

lasso

A **lasso** is a rope of hemp or rawhide with a running knot used to catch cattle and horses.

last

Last means coming after all the others.

This is the **last** part of my homework. I have finished all the rest.

late

Late means coming after the usual time period. I try never to be **late** for school. I get there fifteen minutes early every day.

laugh

When I saw the clown pour water into his pants, I **laughed** out loud. It was the funniest thing I'd ever seen.

laundry

1. A **laundry** is a place where washing and ironing of clothing is done.

2. **Laundry** is the clothing or other things that are to be washed or have already been washed.

law

Law is the rule that people agree to obey so they will be safe and treated fairly in their dealings with each other.

lay

1. Please **lay** the book on the desk. Please put it there.
2. The hens will **lay** a dozen eggs by morning.

lazy

I didn't want to clean my room today. I was feeling very **lazy.**

lead

1. **Lead** is a heavy, soft, bluish-gray metal. Some pipes used when building houses are made of **lead.**
2. The majorette will **lead** the parade. She will be the first person who starts marching. Everyone else will follow her.

(This word is pronounced differently for each meaning. Please ask your teacher or your parents how these words sound.)

laundry

leaf

A **leaf** is part of a tree, bush or flower. **Leaves** are thin and flat and often green. In the summer, tree **leaves** are green. In the autumn, they change colors and, by winter, they fall off the trees.

leaves

learn

Learning means getting to know about something. We go to school to **learn** how to read, to write, and to do arithmetic.

least

Least means the smallest amount. In the story of The Three Bears, Baby Bear had the **least** amount of porridge. Mama and Papa Bear each had more porridge than Baby Bear.

leather

Leather is the skin of certain animals, especially cattle. **Leather** is used for making things such as shoes, handbags, and clothing.

leave

1. The train will **leave** the station at four o'clock to go to Washington.
2. Please **leave** the puppies alone. Do not touch them.

left

Part of the verb **leave.**

1. The train **left** at four o'clock. It reached our town at five o'clock.

2. **Left** is a direction. If you face toward the north and your arms are pointed straight out from your sides, the arm pointing west is the **left** arm.

leg

The **leg** is part of the body. **Legs** hold the body up and make it possible for people and animals to walk and run.

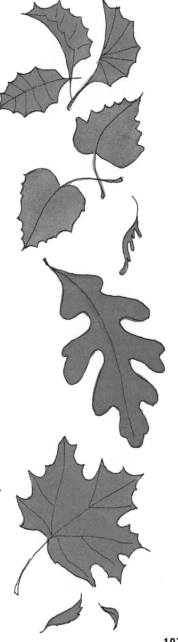

length

A **length** is a measurement. **Length** tells how long something is.

1. The dining room table is sixty inches in **length.**
2. The **length** of the movie was two hours and fifteen minutes.

letter

less

Less means a smaller amount.

Yesterday we ate two eggs for breakfast. Today we ate only one egg. We ate **less** today than yesterday.

let

Let means to allow.

Mom will **let** me go out after lunch.

letter

1. Letters are symbols used to make words. There are twenty-six **letters** in the English alphabet. They are:
A,B,C,D,E,F,G,H,I,J,K,L,M,N,O,P,Q,R,S,T,U,V,W,X,Y,Z.

2. A **letter** is a written message sent from one place to another.

lick

Lick means to pass the tongue over something. Did you ever see a kitten **lick** milk from a bowl.

lick

lie

1. Lie means to say something that is not true. He told a **lie.**

2. I will **lie** on my bed until I fall asleep.

life

Life is the time between birth and death. All my **life** I have lived in the city. I was born here and I have never moved away.

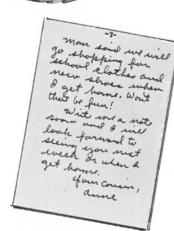

lift

Lift means to bring upward from the ground. Please **lift** your coat off the floor. It has fallen off the hanger.

lighthouse

A **lighthouse** is a tower with a powerful light at the top that shines out to sea so that ships will see it and avoid coming too near the rocky shore at night.

lightning

Lightning is a flash of light in the sky. It is electricity that moves from clouds to the earth or to other clouds.

like

1. I **like** candy. It pleases me.
2. I would **like** to go to the movies.

line

1. A **line** is a continuous mark which can be either straight or curved. Notebooks have blue **lines** in them.
2. Sometimes when you go to the movies, there are lots of people waiting. Everyone has to form a **line** to get into the theatre. People **line** up one behind the other.

lip

Lips are part of the face. **Lips** are the soft parts at the edge of the opening of the mouth.

liquid

A **liquid** is something that flows and can be poured. Water, milk, soda all are liquids.

lighthouse

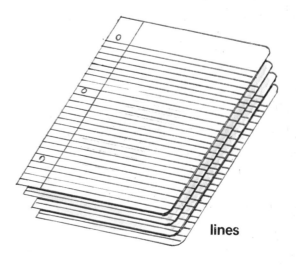

lines

lips

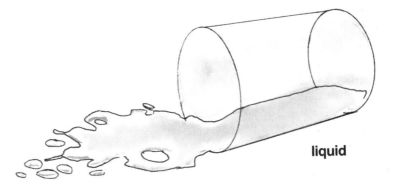

liquid

list

A **list** is several names, numbers or words set down on paper one after another. Some kids **list** all the presents they want Santa Claus to bring them and then send their **lists** to the North Pole.

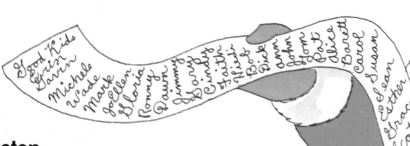

listen

Listen means to pay attention in order to hear.

Children in school **listen** to their teacher in order to hear what she is telling them.

live

1. Some people **live** in the city and some have their homes in the country. Where do you **live?**
2. Leaves **live** when they are on the tree. In the autumn, they dry up and fall off the tree. They are dead.

lives

Lives means more than one life. I want to spend my life as a doctor; my brother wants to teach. Work is important in both our **lives.**

list

load

We had many things to move to our new house. We took three **loads** of things to the house on Sunday. We **loaded** up our car and the trailer each time.

loaf

A **loaf** is a portion of bread. Bread dough is mixed and then separated into separate pieces called **loaves.** For sandwiches, each **loaf** of bread is cut into thin slices.

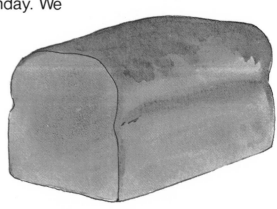

loaf

loan

A **loan** is that which is borrowed. I forgot my lunch. Will you please **lend** me money so I can buy a sandwich. I will repay the **loan** tomorrow.

lock

A **lock** is used to keep something closed. Most doors have **locks.** Cars have **locks.** Keys are usually used to open **locks.**

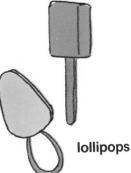

lollipops

lock

lollipop

A **lollipop** is a kind of candy. **Lollipops** are hard candies on sticks. **Lollipops** taste sweet and are licked until they are gone.

long

1. I have to go twenty miles to school. That is a **long** way from my house.
2. I **long** for a new bike. That means I want it very much and I think about it all the time.

look

If you want to see something wonderful, **look** out the window. The snow is falling and making everything white.

loose

1. Someone left the gate open and the dog is **loose.** He ran away.
2. My new shoes were too **loose** and they were falling off. The shoemaker fixed them so they are not too **loose** for me.

lose

1. Do not **lose** your book. Be sure to put it where you can find it.
2. If you play a game and you **lose,** don't be angry. Try harder, and maybe you will win the next time.

lost

Lost is part of the verb **lose.**

1. If you have **lost** your book, tell your teacher right away.
2. My team won the game; yours **lost.**

loud

One night when I was in bed I heard a **loud** noise. Someone was shooting off fireworks and there was a roar as each one exploded.

love

Love is a good feeling. When you care very much for someone and you like to be with them and you wish good things for them, that is **love.**

Children and parents **love** each other.

low

1. That sweater does not cost much. It has a very **low** price.
2. The coat rack in school is **low** so that it is not too high for small children to reach.

luck

The words that I had to spell for my test were the same ones I studied last night. That was good **luck.** I knew the answers.

lumber

Lumber is wood that is cut into pieces of certain size boards.

lumberjack

Lumberjack is the name given to the person that cuts down trees in order to make lumber. **Lumberjacks** use saws to cut trees down.

lump

She got hit on the head with a volleyball. It made a large **lump** on her head. The **lump** was hard and it stuck up on her head.

lumberjack

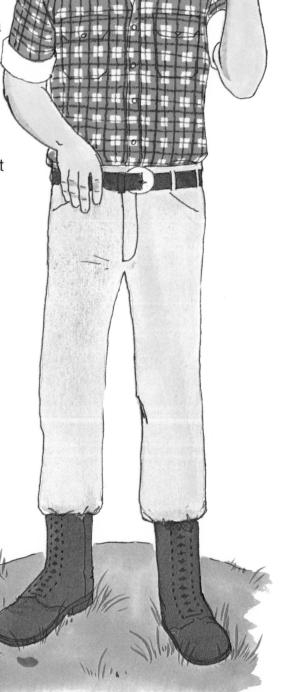

Can you name the things on this page that begin with the letter M? See answers at bottom of page.

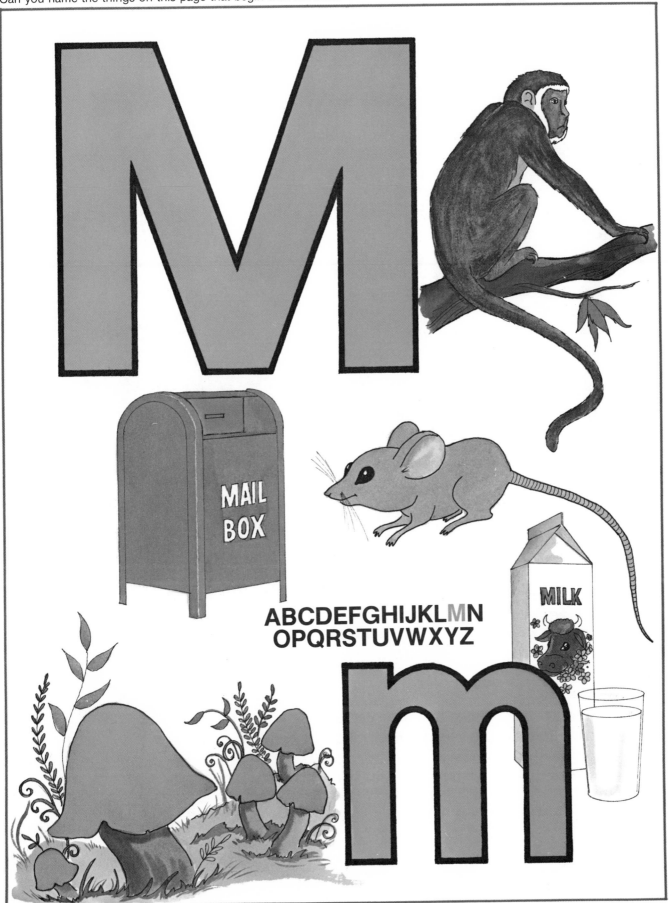

ABCDEFGHIJKLMN
OPQRSTUVWXYZ

MAIL BOX

MILK

mad

My little sister wrote all over my homework. I was really angry with her. She made me **mad.**

made

Made is part of the verb **make.**

Mom and I will **make** cookies. We mix flour and sugar and eggs and other things and then bake them. We **made** thirty-six cookies.

magic

Magic is a way of making it seem that things happen that don't seem possible. In the story of Cinderella, the fairy godmother uses magic to change a pumpkin into a royal coach.

magician

A **magician** is a person who performs magic. **Magicians** make it seem that they can do things like pulling a rabbit out of a hat and turning a lady into a tiger.

magnet

A **magnet** is a piece of steel or iron to which other metals are attracted.

mail

1. Mail is the letters or packages that are sent or delivered through the postal service.
2. I **mailed** a birthday card to my friend today. It will get to her tomorrow.

make

1. I **make** hot chocolate by mixing cocoa and milk together and then heating it on the stove.
2. Mom wants me to **make** my bed before I go to school. I pull up the blankets and make the sheets smooth and neat.

magician

male
People are either **male** or female. Men and boys are **male.**

man
A **man** is a male human being. Boys grow up to be **men.**

man

manage
Manage means to guide, control and direct. Horses, to be fine racers or jumpers, have to be carefully **managed** to be sure they learn to do the right things at the right time.

many
Many means a large number. There are **many** trees in the forest.

map
A **map** is a kind of picture that shows where places are. **Maps** guide travelers to their destination. **Maps** show where roads are and what places can be reached along the roads. A **map** of the world shows where the continents and the oceans are.

map

maple
A **maple** is a kind of tree. **Maple** trees give off sticky sap that can be turned into **maple** sugar.

marble
1. Marble is a hard stone that can be polished to a smooth shiny surface and used for furniture and other things.
2. Marbles are small round glass balls that are used to play games.

marbles

March

March is the third month of the year. It comes between February and April. There are thirty-one days in **March.**

march

March means to walk in a special, careful way. In parades, the **marchers** all **march** along with the same size steps.

mark

1. Your **marks** in school tell how well you have done. 100% or "A" are the best **marks** in school.
2. There was a purple **mark** on the floor that didn't wash off. That was where grape juice spilled.

marry

When a man and a woman agree to join together and share their lives, they **marry.** They go to a priest, minister, rabbi, or judge and are **married** according to the laws of their state. They become husband and wife.

marsh

The **marsh** is a very wet land area. Certain animals and birds and insects live in **marshes.** There are high grasses in **marshes.**

marshmallow

A **marshmallow** is a kind of candy. **Marshmallows** are soft, puffy, white, sweet candies.

match

1. A **match** is a short thin piece of wood or paper with a chemical on the top that will flame up if it is rubbed on a rough surface.
2. Did you ever go out with socks that didn't **match?** Were they different colors?

marching

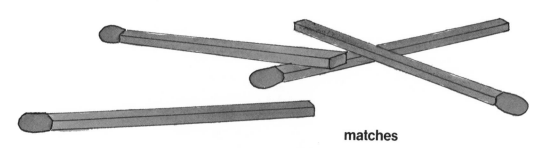

matches

mattress

The **mattress** is the part of the bed that people sleep on.

Mattresses consist of a cloth outer covering filled with foam rubber or other soft material. Sheets and blankets go over the **mattress.**

May

May is the fifth month of the year. There are thirty-one days in **May. May** comes between April and June.

may

1. You **may** go home now. You are allowed to go.
2. I **may** go skating today. I'm not sure yet.

maybe

Maybe means perhaps.

Maybe I can go with you. I am not sure yet.

me

Give it to **me!** Put it in my hand.

May

meadow

Meadows are grassy areas of land. Cows like to graze in **meadows.**

meal

A **meal** is the food we eat at a particular time of the day. Breakfast, lunch and dinner are **meals.**

meadow

117

mean

1. Big and large **mean** the same thing. When you say something is big or it is large you have the same idea of that object. The words have the same **meaning.**
2. It will **mean** a lot to me to make the football team.
3. We think the teacher is **mean** because he gives us so much homework.

meant

Meant is part of the verb **mean.** I wore my green sweater by mistake. I **meant** to wear the red one.

measure

When you go to the doctor for a checkup she takes your **measurements.** Using a scale, she **measures** your height and your weight.

medicine

Medicine is made from plants and other things. If they are sick, people use **medicine** to make them better.

melt

Ice is frozen water. If you put an ice cube in the sun it will change from a solid substance into a pool of water. It will **melt**.

memory

Do you remember all about your last birthday? If so, you have a good **memory.**

measuring

men

Men means more than one man.

There were two **men** waiting for the bus.

mess

When your toys and clothes are all over your room in a pile, your room is a **mess.** When you clean the **mess,** your room will be neat and orderly.

message

A **message** is a way of getting ideas from one person to another. A letter, a telegram, or a telephone call may be a **message.**

met

Met is part of the word **meet.**

We **met** each other at the movies. We agreed to **meet** at one o'clock.

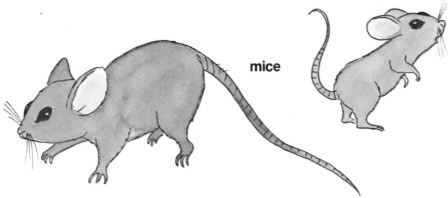

mice

mice

Mice means more than one mouse.
Mice are very small animals of the rodent family.

might

Might is part of the verb **may.**

I **might** have been able to go swimming today if the sun had come out.

mile

A **mile** is an amount of distance. There are 5,280 feet in a mile. Two-thirds of a mile is about the same as one kilometer.

Mm

million
A **million** is a very large number that is equal to one thousand thousands. It is written 1,000,000.

mind
The **mind** is the part of a human being that thinks. When you have an idea or a dream, your **mind** is working.

mine
This bicycle belongs to me. It is **mine.**

minus
In mathematics, if you want to subtract the number two from the number 10, you show the problem as ten **minus** two equals 8 or 10-2=8.

minus

miss
1. If you get to the airport five minutes after the plane has left, you have **missed** the flight.
2. When you are away from home for a long time, you may **miss** your parents. You wish you could see them and talk to them.

mistake
I made a **mistake** when I told you I would be home right after school. I have to go to football practice for an hour.

mix
Mix means to put several things together in one place and combine them. When you make pancakes you **mix** flour and eggs and milk in a bowl and stir them.

mixing

model

A **model** is a small copy of a larger object. Children like to make **model** airplanes and doll house **models. Models** can be made of clay, paper, wood, etc.

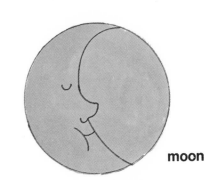

moon

Mom, Mommy

Mom or **Mommy** is the name some children call their **mothers.**

monster

moment

A **moment** is a very short small amount of time. Has anyone ever asked you to hold on a **moment** on the telephone? That means they want you to stay on the phone for a minute or so.

Monday

Monday is the second day of the week. **Monday** comes between Sunday and Tuesday.

money

Money is used to buy things. Coins and paper bills are used for **money.** Gold, silver and other valuables are sometimes used as money, too.

monster

In stories, **monsters** are huge, imaginary, frightening creatures. They may be either animals or people.

mood

A **mood** is the way people feel at different times. Sometimes we wake up in a happy **mood.** Sometimes we are in a grumpy **mood.** Then we don't feel too happy.

moon

A **moon** is a heavenly body that revolves around a planet. From earth we see our **moon** as a bright ball in the sky at night. The sun's reflection causes the **moon** to appear as if it is lighted.

more

More means a greater amount.

I have six marbles. I would like to have eight. Will you please give me two **more**?

most

Most means the greatest in any way.

Mr. and Mrs. Smith have four children. Three of their children go to school; one doesn't. **Most** of their children go to school.

moth

A **moth** is an insect with wings. **Moths** are different from butterflies. They have stouter bodies, smaller wings, and are not as colorful.

moths

mother

A **mother** is a female who has given birth to a child.

motor

A **motor** is a machine that causes things to move by changing energy to motion. Automobiles have **motors** that use gasoline to make it possible to drive them.

mouth

The **mouth** is the opening through which people and animals take in food.

move

1. Cars stop when the traffic light is red. When the light turns green all the cars start to **move.**

2. When our grandparents came to live with us, the whole family **moved** to a new house.

mother

movie

A **movie** is a motion picture. **Movies** are a way of showing people and things moving by using special cameras, film, projectors, and screens.

much

1. There was **much** happiness in my house when my baby sister was born.
2. When you want to know the price of anything you can ask "How **much** is this?"

mud

Mud is earth that is wet and soft.

mud

multiply

In arithmetic, **multiplying** means adding a number to itself any number of times that you wish. For example, 3 **multiplied** by 4 is 3+3+3+3=12 or 3x4=12 or 3 times 4 is 12.

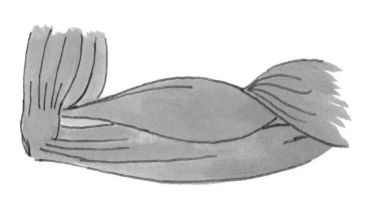

muscle

muscle

A **muscle** is part of the body. **Muscles** are stringlike fibers under the skin that stretch to make it possible for us to move.

must

It is a rule in my house. We **must** keep our rooms clean. We have to do it.

mustard

Mustard is a powder or paste made from mustard seeds. **Mustard** is used to make certain foods taste better. Some **mustard** is hot tasting.

my
When I want to say that something belongs to me, I say "That is **my** book … **my** dog … **my** house, etc."

myself
I will walk the dog **myself.** You don't have to do it.

mystery
A **mystery** is something that is not fully understood.

Why my sister likes to go to school is a **mystery** to me.

mystery

Can you name the things on this page that begin with the letters N or O? See answers at bottom of page.

Nn

nail

1. The **nail** is the thin, hard substance that grows on the upper side of fingers and toes.

2. Nails are round, thin, pointed pieces of metal that are pushed through pieces of wood to hold them together.

nails

name

A **name** is what a thing is called. Everything has a **name.** Each person has a **name** that tells who he is. Ann is a girl's **name**; Robert is a boy's **name**.

narrow

narrow

Narrow means not very wide.

There was a **narrow** opening in the fence for the kids to get through.

natural

Natural means something that is made or caused by nature. Hurricanes and floods are called **natural** disasters.

nature

Nature refers to all the forces at work in the universe. All people, plants, animals, the sun, moon, and planets are parts of **nature.**

near

Near means not very far from. If you live **near** your friend, you can probably walk to his house very quickly.

neat

A room is **neat** if everything is in the place that it belongs. The room is orderly.

need

I **need** two tires for my bicycle. I have money to buy one tire, but I still **need** another one.

neither

Neither means not one or the other. There are two kinds of soda. **Neither** one is the kind I like.

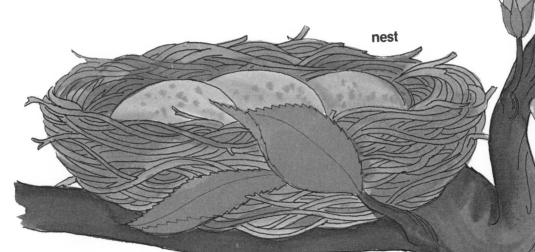

nest

nest

A **nest** is the place that a bird builds and uses to keep its eggs until they are hatched and where the young birds stay until they are old enough to care for themselves.

never

Never means not ever, at no time.

I **never** want to go to that place again.

new

1. There was a **new** boy in class today. He just moved to town.

2. My **new** house is being built now.

newspaper

A **newspaper** is a series of printed pages containing pictures and stories that tell people about the things that are happening in their town or in the world.

next

This year Jimmy is in the first grade. **Next** year he will be in the second grade.

Nn

nice

Nice means pleasing or kind.

1. This is a **nice** sweater. It is my favorite color.

2. My teacher is very **nice.** She is kind to the kids and is lots of fun.

nice

nightmare

A **nightmare** is a scary dream.

no

1. When you don't want something, you say "**No**, thank you," when it is offered. When you don't want to go somewhere you say "**No**, thank you," when you are invited.

2. The car is going as fast as it can go. We can go **no** faster.

nobody

Nobody means not one person. I went to my friend's house but **nobody** was home.

nod

Nod means to gently bend your head up and down. If you want to agree with someone, you might **nod** your head.

noise

Noise is a sound of any kind. When dogs bark, they make a lot of **noise.**

north

North is a direction. If you face the sun as it sets, **north** is to the right.

north

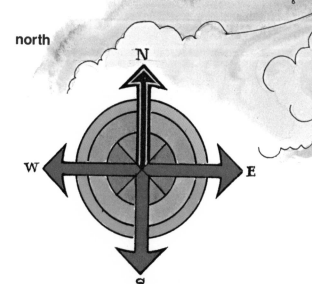

nose

The **nose** is part of the body. It is on the face. We breathe air and smell things through our **noses.**

not

Sometimes it snows in winter. It does **not** snow in summer.

nothing

Nothing means not anything.

There was **nothing** I could do to finish my homework on time. There was just too much.

nose

November

November is the eleventh month of the year. It is the month between October and December. There are thirty days in **November.**

now

Now means at the present time.

Let's go **now.** It is time to go.

nut

A **nut** is a fruit that grows inside a hard, woody shell. Pecans, walnuts and almonds are **nuts.**

nuts

oak

The **oak** is a tree. Acorns are the fruit of the **oak** tree. The wood of the **oak** tree is used for making furniture.

oar

An **oar** is a long piece of wood that is shaped round and narrow at one end where the rower will hold it, and broad and flat at the end that enters the water. **Oars** are used to row and steer boats.

oar

obey

Obey means to do as you are told and to act according to rules.

Children **obey** their parents; citizens of a country **obey** the laws of that country.

object

1. Objects are all things you can see or touch. All the toys in your room are **objects**.

objects

2. Object means the reason for, the purpose. The **object** of going to school is to learn.

o'clock

O'clock means of or by the clock. When we say two **o'clock,** it means that according to a clock it is two hours past noon or midnight.

October

October is the tenth month of the year. It comes after September and before November. There are thirty-one days in **October.**

OCTOBER

October

of

1. Those drawings are the work **of** the second grade pupils.

2. There are six **of** one painting; seven **of** the other.

3. The gerbil cage is made **of** plastic. It is a plastic box.

off

Off means not on.

1. Please get the dog **off** the bed. He belongs on the floor.

2. The telephone and lights in the house are **off.** They are not working.

offer

Mom **offered** to take the kids in my class to the beach. She said we could go on a Saturday morning.

often

Often means happening many times.

We go to the movies **often.** We go every week on Saturday.

old

Old means not new; not young.

1. I've had my bike for eight years. It is an **old** bike.

2. My dog is fourteen years **old.** He is an **old** dog.

on

1. The cat is sitting **on** the piano.

2. My sister was angry at me. She hit me **on** purpose.

3. Before you try to drive a car, make sure the brake is not **on.**

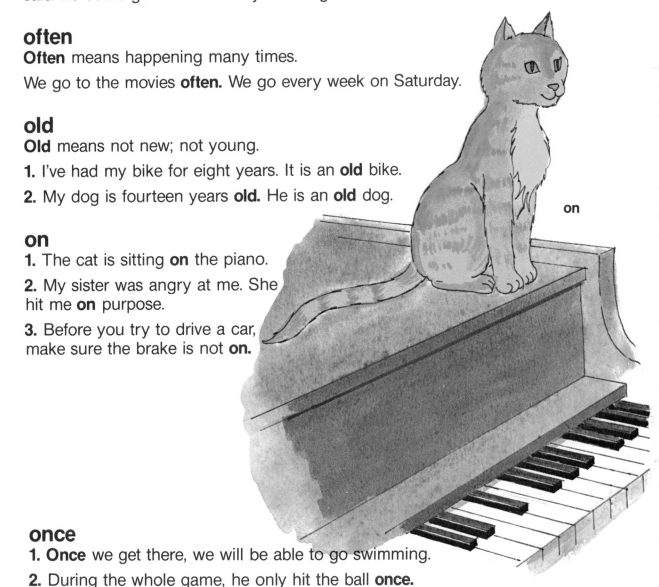

on

once

1. Once we get there, we will be able to go swimming.

2. During the whole game, he only hit the ball **once.**

one

One is a number between zero and two. It refers to a single person or thing.

There is **one** day left in this month. Then a new month will start.

Oo

only

1. I have **only** one pet. Mom won't let me have more.

2. I will go **only** if you go too. There is no other reason for me to go.

open

1. If you leave the door **open**, the mosquitoes will get in.

2. We will be at the movie at one o'clock when it **opens**.

or

Do you want vanilla **or** chocolate ice cream? I'll take either the vanilla **or** the chocolate.

orchestra

An **orchestra** is a group of musicians playing various musical instruments at the same time, following the music written by the composer.

order

1. Mom called the bakery and **ordered** a birthday cake. It will be ready for my birthday.

2. The soldier received an **order** from the general. He was told to drive a truck across the country.

3. If a room is neat and everything is in place, it is in **order**.

ostrich

An **ostrich** is a very large bird with long legs and a long neck. **Ostriches** have two toes on each foot. They can't fly but they can run very fast.

other

1. I don't want this hat. I like the **other** one better.

2. Every **other** year we go on a skiing vacation. We didn't go last year, so we will be going this year.

ostrich

ounce

An **ounce** is an amount of weight. There are sixteen **ounces** in a pound.

our, ours

This is **our** house. It belongs to **our** family. It is **ours**.

out

1. My dog likes to go **out** four times a day. He likes me to walk him around the neighborhood.

2. They say we are running **out** of oil and that it will all be gone in years to come.

oval

An **oval** is a shape. It is nearly the same shape as the outline of an egg.

ovals

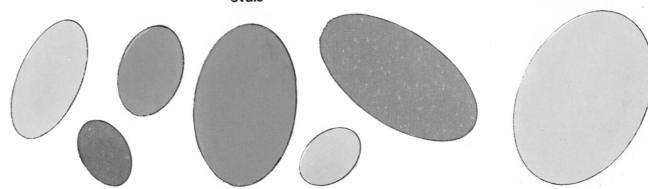

over

1. The bird flew **over** the house.

2. Five goes into seven one time, with two left **over**.

3. When school's **over,** we go on vacation.

4. We will be away **over** the holidays.

5. Can you stay **over** at my house today.

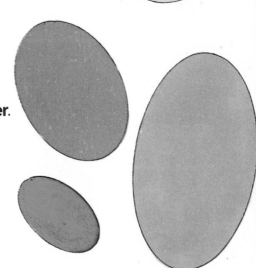

own

Own means belonging to oneself.

1. I will use my **own** pen.

2. I would like to **own** two ponies. When I earn enough money I will buy them.

Can you name the things on this page that begin with the letter P? See answers at bottom of page.

ABCDEFGHIJKLMNO**P**QRSTUVWXYZ

pack

1. When you go hiking, you carry a **pack** on your back that holds all the things you need.

2. When you go away on vacation, you **pack** a suitcase with clothes in it.

package

At Christmas, I got a **package** from my friend. It was all wrapped and tied up prettily and inside was a new book for me to read.

paddle

A **paddle** is a short oar with a broad blade at one end, or both ends, that is used for canoeing.

page

A **page** is one side of a piece of paper. Newspapers, books, and magazines all have pages.

paid

Paid is part of the verb **pay**.

I brought money to the store and **paid** for three ice cream cones.

pail

A **pail** is a container for carrying water or some other liquid. **Pails** can be made of wood or plastic or metal.

pain

If a part of your body is hurt, you will feel **pain** at the spot where you were hurt. If you get sunburned you will feel **pain** on your skin.

pack

pail

Pp

pair
Pair means two things that are similar in form.

I need a new **pair** of socks.

Will you get me that **pair** of scissors?

palace
A **palace** is a large and beautiful house that was built for a king or queen or emperor to live in.

palm
The **palm** is the inner surface of the hand from the wrist to where the fingers start.

pancake
A **pancake** is a kind of food. **Pancakes** are thin, flat cakes that are cooked in a pan or on a griddle. They are made from flour, eggs, and milk and taste good with butter and maple syrup.

paper
Paper is a substance used for writing on, printing on, for wrapping and for many other purposes. **Paper** is made from wood.

parachute
A **parachute** is made of wide sheets of cloth and straps or lines. **Parachutes** are used by people who jump from airplanes so that they will come down through the air slowly enough that they will not be hurt.

parade
A **parade** is a public event. At **parades,** people march along the street, one behind the other to celebrate a special occasion. Sometimes they play musical instruments or have floats.

palace

parent
A **parent** is a father or a mother.

part
The hands, arms, and head are all **parts** of the body. Each one is a **part** of the whole body.

pass
1. If I do well and **pass** my exams, I will go on to the next grade.

2. The salt is down at your end of the table. Will you please **pass** it to me.

3. On our trip through the countryside, we **passed** fields with cows and horses in them.

past
The **past** is the time that has gone by. In the **past** there were no airplanes and people traveled on railroads and ships and in carriages or on horseback.

patch

patch
A **patch** is a piece of cloth sewn on a garment to repair it.

path
A **path** is a narrow area in a woods which is cleared by walking over it many times.

paw
A paw is the foot of an animal that has claws or nails.

paws

137

pay

Pay means to give money or other valuables in exchange for something wanted or needed.

We work to earn money to **pay** for food, clothing and a place to live.

pea

A **pea** is a food. **Peas** are round, green seeds that are very good for people to eat. We eat **peas** as a vegetable.

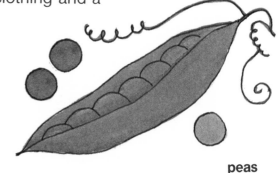

peas

peanut butter

Peanut butter is a paste made by grinding up roasted peanuts. **Peanut butter** on bread is very good to eat.

pedal

A **pedal** is something you press with your foot to cause some action.

The **pedal** is the part of a bicycle that you put your foot on to make the bicycle move.

pen, pencil

Pens and **pencils** are used for writing. A **pen** is a long, thin, piece of wood or plastic with a place to hold ink and a point on it for writing. **Pencils** have a strip of graphite encased in wood or metal that can be sharpened and used for writing or drawing.

people

People are human beings. They are men, women and children.

perfect

Today is a **perfect** day. The sun is shining, the sky is blue, the air is clear and cool. Everything is exactly right.

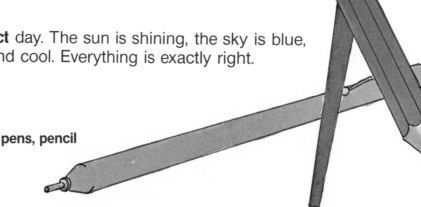

pens, pencil

perhaps

Perhaps means maybe.

If you get here on time, **perhaps** we can go to the amusement park.

person

A **person** is a human being. Men, women, and children are **persons**.

pet

A **pet** is a tame animal usually kept in the house because it provides fun and pleasure to its owner.

phone

Phone is a short way to say **'telephone.'** A **phone** is a device that makes it possible for people to talk to each other even when they are at a great distance from each other.

pick

1. In the autumn, it is fun to **pick** the apples and other fruits from the trees. After they are **picked**, they are put in baskets and sold.

2. Dad said I could chose white or blue paint for my room. I **picked** blue.

picture

1. I like to take **pictures** with my camera. **Pictures** help me remember where I have been because they show me people and places that I may have forgotten.
2. I drew a **picture** of my teacher with watercolors. The **picture** looked just like her.

pie

Pie is a food. **Pies** have thin breadlike bottom crusts; then fillings of fruit or meat in the middle and another crust on top. The whole **pie** is baked in the oven.

picture

phone

pet

139

piece

We cut the cake into eight equal **pieces.** I ate one **piece** and left the other **pieces** for the rest of the family.

pile

A **pile** is a collection of things lying one on top of the other.

When the children came in from the snow, they dropped their boots and coats and made a big wet **pile** on the floor.

pin

A **pin** is a thin piece of metal, wood, or plastic with a sharp point that is used to hold things together. Metal **pins** are used when sewing to hold the pieces of cloth together until they are sewn.

pins

pinch

Pinch means to squeeze between the fingers.

Naughty children sometimes **pinch** each other when they are angry. **Pinching** hurts!

pint

A **pint** is an amount of liquid that is equal to one half a quart. Milk at school often comes in **pint** containers.

pipe

A **pipe** is a hollow tube made of wood, metal or concrete to carry liquids, gas or steam.

pirate

A **pirate** is a robber who steals the property of others on the high seas. **Pirates** travel the oceans even today in all kinds of boats.

pirate

pitcher

1. **A pitcher** may be used to hold liquids.

2. In baseball, the player who throws the ball is the **pitcher**.

place

A **place** is where any one person or any thing can be found. Cities, towns, houses, and even the corners of your room are **places**.

plan

A **plan** means thinking about something you expect to do to be sure it comes out right. If you **plan** to go to the movies on Saturday, you have to check what time the movie will start, how much it will cost, and find friends to go with you.

plant

A **plant** is part of the vegetable kingdom. All things that grow in the ground are **plants**. Flowers, trees and all the vegetables we eat are **plants**.

plastic

Plastic is a chemical material which, when heated up and put under pressure, can be made into many shapes. Many things, including toys, are made of **plastic**.

plate

1. A **plate** is a round, smooth, almost flat piece of pottery, porcelain or plastic from which food is eaten.

2. In baseball, the home base is also called home **plate**.

please

1. To **please** means to make happy, to satisfy.

2. We say "**Please**," when we want someone to do something for us.

pitcher

pitcher

Pp

plus

Three **plus** six is equal to nine. 3 + 6 = 9.
Three added to six is nine.

pocket

A **pocket** is a small cloth pouch
sewn inside a part of clothing. We
keep things we need, such as
money, toys or candy with us in
our **pockets**.

pockets

poem

A **poem** is a group of words put together in a special way
to give the reader a word picture that tells how the poet felt
about something. **Poems** can be very sad or very beautiful
or happy.

poet

A **poet** is a person who writes a poem.

point

1. A **point** is the end of, or the mark made by the end of,
a sharp object such as a pen, pencil or nail.

2. If you lift your arm and put your finger straight ahead
you are **pointing** at something.

point

pole

A **pole** is a long, thin piece of
wood or metal. There used to be
barber **poles** outside stores where
haircuts were given.

poor

Poor means not having enough food, clothing, money, or
other needed things.

pop

Pop is a short, explosive sound. Fireworks make **popping** noises.

popcorn

Popcorn is a food. **Popcorn** is good for you and it tastes good. It is made from a special kind of corn kernels that are cooked quickly in a hot pot until they start exploding into puffy white pieces.

popcorn

porpoise

porpoise

A **porpoise** is an animal that lives in the sea. **Porpoises** are usually five to eight feet long. They are blackish in color on top and paler underneath. **Porpoises**, sometimes called dolphins, have blunt, rounded snouts.

possible

Possible means something that may be, or may happen. It is **possible** that it will snow today on the mountaintops.

pound

A **pound** is an amount of weight. There are sixteen ounces in a **pound** or approximately 450 grams.

pour

1. It has been raining hard all day. It is **pouring** rain.

2. Please lift the bottle of milk and **pour** some into the glass.

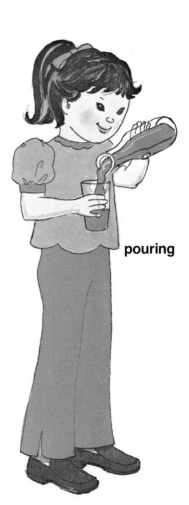

pouring

powder

Powder is very tiny pieces of ground up material. Cocoa beans are ground into a **powder** so they can be mixed with sugar and other things to make chocolate.

practice

If you want to learn to do something very well, you **practice** by doing it over and over again. To play any sport well, you have to **practice** a lot.

prepare

Prepare means to get ready. In the morning you **prepare** yourself to go to school. You get up, get dressed and have breakfast.

presents

present

1. A **present** is a gift. On her birthday, Jeannie got **presents** from all her friends.

2. Present means at this time, now. Today is the **present**, yesterday is the past and tomorrow is the future.

3. At roll-call time in school, the teacher calls a student's name. If he is there, he will say, "**Present.**"

pretend

Pretend means to make believe. When Mom and Dad check to see if I am sleeping at night, I keep my eyes shut and **pretend** to be asleep.

pretty

Pretty means nice looking. My baby sister looks very **pretty** to me.

price

The **price** is the amount one has to spend to buy something.

prince

A **prince** is a man or a boy who is the son of a king or queen.

prince

144

princess

A **princess** is a woman or girl who is the daughter of a king or queen.

print

1. Printing is a way of writing the letters of the alphabet, in which each letter is written separately, and letters are not attached to each other. Children learn to **print** before they learn script.

2. Machines that put letters on paper for books, magazines, and newspapers are called **printing** presses.

prize

A **prize** is a reward for winning. In contests, there are usually **prizes** for the winners.

probably

If I leave school at three o'clock and run all the way, I will **probably** get home in time for my piano lesson at 3:15.

problem

1. A **problem** is a question that is to be answered. The math teacher gave us six math **problems** to do for homework.

2. Problem is something that is a worry. My friend and I had a **problem** getting air in our bicycle tires. We couldn't find any air pumps.

promise

Mom **promised** to bake some chocolate cookies. I know she will do it because she never breaks her **promises.**

protect

Protect means to keep from danger. Football is a dangerous game. Football players use heavy padding and helmets to **protect** their heads and bodies while they are playing.

princess

proud

When you do something well, you are **proud** of yourself. You know you do a good job, and that feels good.

pry

Pry means to lift or move by force. To **pry** open a can of paint, a strong screwdriver can be put into the area between the edge of the can and the top of the can and, when pushed down, it will lift up the cover.

puddle

A **puddle** is a small amount of water or other liquid that collects on the ground.

pull

To **pull** means to tug at with force. My class had a tug-of-war. There were two teams with twelve children on each team. We all **pulled** on a rope until one team **pulled** the other team over the line.

puddle

pumpkin

A **pumpkin** is a large, orange-colored fruit that grows on a vine. **Pumpkins** are made into jack-o-lanterns on Halloween and can also be cooked to make **pumpkin** pie.

pup, puppy

A **pup**, or **puppy**, is a young dog or seal.

puppet

A **puppet** is a small figure that looks like a person or animal that is moved by hand or cords. **Puppets** are usually made of wood or plastic and cloth.

puppets

push

When using revolving doors, you walk in, put your hands on the door, and **push** it. It moves and you walk out the other side.

put

After Eddie finishes his homework, he gathers all his books and **puts** them in his schoolbag. Yesterday he **put** four books into the bag.

puzzle

Puzzles are games. Jigsaw **puzzles** are pictures on board that have been cut and broken into many small pieces. **Puzzles** are fun to put back together again.

puzzle

Can you name the things on this page that begin with the letters Q or R? See answers at bottom of page.

ABCDEFGHIJKLMN
OPQRSTUVWXYZ

quart

Quart is an amount of liquid. There are thirty-two ounces in a **quart**; two pints in a **quart**; and four **quarts** in a gallon.

quarter

1. In American money, a **quarter** is a thin silver-colored coin. It is equal to twenty-five cents.

2. A **quarter** is the same as one fourth of anything. If you cut a cake into four equal parts, each piece is one **quarter** of the cake.

quarter

queen

A **queen** is the woman, or the wife of the king, who is the person that rules a kingdom.

question

If you want to know something, you ask a **question**. Most **questions** start with one of these words—who, what, where, when, why or how.

quick

Quick means fast. The **quick** kitten jumped on the ball of yarn before I was able to reach it.

quiet

Quiet means little or no noise. At school we are not allowed to talk during class. It is very **quiet**.

race

A **race** is a contest to see who can go fastest. There are running **races** and boat **races** and many, many more kinds of **races**.

quiet

raft

A **raft** is made up of logs, planks or other pieces of lumber that are tied together so they will float on water.

rain

Rain is water that falls from the clouds onto the earth in drops. **Rain** is needed so that plants of all kinds will grow.

rainbow

A **rainbow** is the wide band of colors sometimes seen in the sky. **Rainbows** are caused by the light from the sun as it hits drops of rain.

rainbow

raincoat

A **raincoat** is a coat that is worn on rainy days because it is made of special cloth that does not let the rain through. **Raincoats** keep the rest of your clothing dry.

raise

1. When you want to speak in class, first you **raise** your hand over your head. The teacher will know you have something to say when she sees your hand **raised**.

2. John's parents are farmers. They **raise** cattle and corn on their farm.

rake

A **rake** is a garden tool used for gathering loose leaves that have fallen from trees.

ranch

A **ranch** is a piece of land used for the raising of cattle. There are many **ranches** in the western part of the United States.

rake

rang

Rang is part of the verb **ring.**

We heard the sound of the new bell as it **rang** from the church steeple. From now on it will **ring** every day.

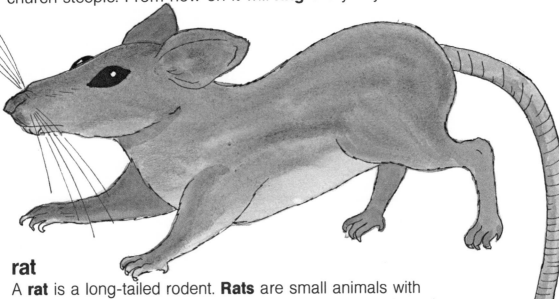

rat

rat

A **rat** is a long-tailed rodent. **Rats** are small animals with gray-brown fur, small ears and teeth that can chew through many things.

reach

1. My new pants are too long. They **reach** all the way to the floor.

2. The ice cream is on the top shelf in the refrigerator. Can you **reach** that far?

read

Read means to understand the meaning of words that are written or printed. Can you **read** this book? It is too hard for me to **read**.

ready

In the morning, after you are dressed and you have had some breakfast, you are **ready** for school.

real

Real means something that is true—not make-believe.

Some candy is made from carob seeds so that it tastes like chocolate, but **real** chocolate is made from cocoa seeds.

really

Really means actually or truly.

I have been up for many hours. I am **really** tired.

reason

I was sick in bed yesterday. That was the **reason** I was not in school.

record

A phonograph **record** is a round, flat disk made of plastic on which sound is **recorded**.

record

reindeer

A **reindeer** is an animal. **Reindeer** are one of many kinds of deer. **Reindeer** are large, four-legged animals with antlers on their heads. It is said that Santa Claus has eight **reindeer**.

reindeer

remember

So that I **remember** my homework, I use a notebook and make a list of all the work I have to do. Then I don't forget anything.

repeat

Repeat means to say or to do something more than once. She didn't hear me the first time. I had to **repeat** myself.

reptile

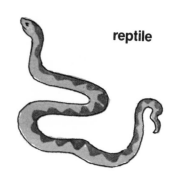

reptile

A **reptile** is an animal that moves on its belly or on short legs. Snakes, alligators and turtles are **reptiles**.

rest

rest

1. When children are small they take a nap so that they can **rest** for a while. When they are not tired any longer they can play again.

2. I am drinking half of my milk now. I'll finish the **rest** at recess time.

return

Return means to give back, to go back.

1. When you have finished reading the book, please **return** it to me.

2. I'll **return** home from school at three o'clock today.

rhinoceros

A **rhinoceros** is a large, thick-skinned gray animal found in Asia and Africa. The **rhinoceros** might have one or two horns on its snout.

rhinoceros

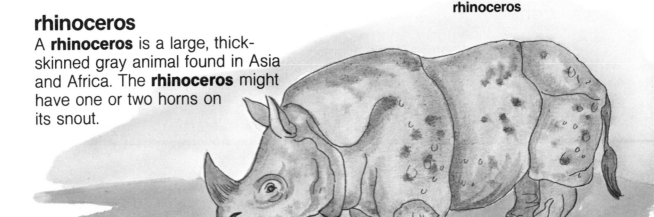

rhyme

Words that **rhyme** have endings that sound the same. For example, brake **rhymes** with make; pen **rhymes** with hen. Sometimes lines of poetry **rhyme** with each other—the final words in each line **rhyme.**

ribbon

A **ribbon** is a narrow band of colored cloth, usually of silk or rayon that is worn as a decoration.

rice

Rice is a food. It is the starchy white or brown grain that comes from a special kind of grass. **Rice** is boiled in water and eaten plain or with meat or vegetables.

ribbons

rich

Rich means having a lot of something that is needed or wanted. **Rich** soil means that things grow very well in it.

ridden

Ridden is part of the verb **ride.**

When she decided to come home, she had **ridden** her horse for two hours.

riddle

A **riddle** is a confusing question, a puzzle that may have a funny answer. "What is black, and white and red all over?" That is the **riddle**. The answer to the **riddle** is: "A blushing zebra."

right

1. If you face north, anything on the east side of you is on the **right** side. **Right** is the opposite of **left**.

2. You answered the questions correctly. You are **right**, not wrong.

3. Rights are things you are allowed to do. In some schools, children have the **right** to go home for lunch if they wish. Not every school allows that.

rings

ring

1. A **ring** is a circular band of metal. People like to wear gold **rings** on their fingers.

2. A **ring** is a bell-like sound. Listen for the **ring** of the telephone.

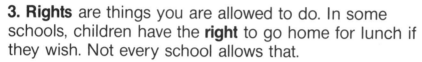

rise

1. In the morning, we **rise** out of bed. We get up from a lying position.

2. Rise means to increase in height. When it rains, the water level in the reservoir **rises** as the water flows in. The water has **risen**.

road

river

A **river** is a large natural stream of water that flows along a special course or channel.

river

road

A **road** is a public passage, usually between towns or cities or parts of towns and cities. Cars, trucks and other vehicles travel on **roads**.

roast

Roasting is a way of cooking. When you **roast** food you put it in a pan in an oven and turn on the heat. The heat **roasts** the food.

rob

Rob means to take something that belongs to someone else. I left my bicycle outside a store and someone took it. It was gone when I came out of the store. I had been **robbed.**

robot

A **robot** is a machine that is made to look something like a human being and can do certain jobs. Some **robots** can even be made so that they are able to talk.

rock

A **rock** is a piece of stone. **Rocks** are part of the earth's surface. Some **rocks** are very pretty. They are hard and large pieces are usually heavy.

rocket

rocket

A **rocket** is a very powerful and noisy device that can be pushed upward into the sky by explosions that take place in the engines. **Rockets** provide the energy to get space vehicles into the sky.

rode

Rode is a part of the verb **ride.**

We **rode** horseback all the way back from the Grand Canyon. I enjoyed the **ride**.

roll

1. A **roll** is a small loaf of bread. Most **rolls** are round. Hot dog **rolls** are long and thin.

2. When you bowl, you **roll** the ball down the alley hoping that it will knock over all ten pins.

roller skate

A **roller skate** is a shoe, or boot or skate that has four small wheels attached to the bottom of it. You can **roller skate** on wooden floors, at roller rinks, or on the sidewalk.

roof

The **roof** is the uppermost part of any house or building.

rooster

rooster

A **rooster** is a male chicken. **Roosters** are birds that say cock-a-doodle-doo in the morning.

rope

A **rope** is a long cord of twisted fibers. **Ropes** are used to tie or fasten things in place.

rose

1. A **rose** is a flower. **Roses** smell very pretty. **Roses** grow on bushes.

2. **Rose** is part of the verb **rise**. The sun will **rise** at six o'clock today. Yesterday it **rose** at 6:03 A.M.

rough

Rough means not smooth. When the water is very **rough** it may be dangerous to swim or to sail.

rose

round

Round is a shape. A ball is **round**. Coins are **round**; the sun, moon and earth are **round**.

row

1. Row means to move a boat on water using oars.

2. At the movies, seats are in **rows**. They are next to each other and set in a straight line from the front to the back of the theatre.

rub

To polish the car, Dad puts wax on a cloth and **rubs** the paint over and over to make it shine.

rubber

Rubber is a material that may be stretched, and, when let go, will go back to its original shape. **Rubber** comes from the juice of a tropical plant. Tires are made of **rubber**.

ruby

A **ruby** is a deep red stone that is found in the earth. **Rubies** are cut and polished and are used in making jewelry.

rule

A **rule** is a kind of law that tells us things we may or may not do.

"No chewing gum" is a **rule** of the school. In baseball, a **rule** is that after three strikes, the batter is out.

run

1. We **run** all the way home from school every day.

2. The street **runs** from east to west.

3. She is going to **run** her father's business when he retires.

run

rung

1. A **rung** is a crosspiece that forms the step on a ladder.

2. Rung is part of the verb **ring**. The school bell should have **rung** at nine o'clock.

Can you name the things on this page that begin with the letter S? See answers at bottom of page.

ABCDEFGHIJKLMN
OPQR**S**TUVWXYZ

sad

Sad means feeling gloomy or unhappy.

I am **sad** today because it is raining and I can't go out.

saddle

Saddle is a seat made of leather that is strapped onto the back of a horse so the rider can sit well.

safe

Safe means not in danger.

The red and green traffic lights at the corners of streets tell when it is **safe** to cross.

same

Same means not different.

That is the **same** teacher we had last year.

sand

Sand is very tiny pieces of rock, or shell, that have been ground into fine grains over a long period of time by wind and water. **Sand** is often found at the beach and in deserts.

sandwich

Sandwich is food that is prepared in a special way. A **sandwich** is two thin slices of bread, with meat, fish, cheese, peanut butter and jelly, or other foods put neatly between them.

Saturday

Saturday is the seventh day of the week. **Saturday** is the day between Friday and Sunday.

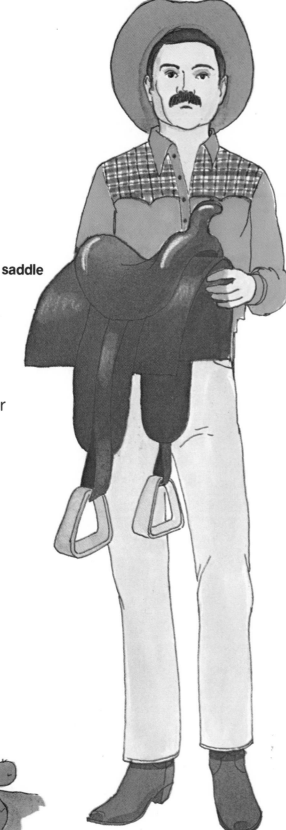

saddle

save

1. When the ice on the pond broke, Jimmy's brother **saved** his life by pulling him out of the water.

2. If you **save** ten cents a day, at the end of the year you will have thirty-six dollars and fifty cents **saved**.

save

saw

1. **Saw** is part of the verb **see**. Yesterday, with my own eyes, I **saw** a monkey dancing.

2. A **saw** is a tool used to cut hard things such as wood, metal, or plastic. **Saws** have sharp edges that cut when moved over the material to be **sawed**.

say

What do you **say** when you answer the telephone? I **say** "Hello!"

scissors

scissors

Scissors are a cutting tool that has two blades with sharp inside edges that move against each other. There are holes at the end of each blade for the fingers to hold the **scissors. Scissors** are most often used to cut paper and cloth.

scratch

When kittens are young, their claws are very sharp, and if you play with them you are likely to be **scratched**. The **scratches** will be long thin cuts in your skin.

sell

When you go to the store, you give the person in the store money and he gives you milk. He **sells** the milk to you. You buy it.

send

Send means to cause a person or thing to go.

1. When I want a message to go from me to my friend, I **send** a letter through the mail.

2. When I was ill, my teacher **sent** me home from school.

September

September is the ninth month of the year. It comes between August and October. There are 30 days in **September**.

set

A **set** is a group of things that look alike or in some way match. A **set** of drums consists of several drums that each produce different sounds but are played together. A **set** of dishes consists of cups, saucers, and plates that have the same design.

sew

Sew means to fasten together with stitches, using a needle and thread. Clothing is **sewn** together. I can **sew** clothes for my doll.

shake

Shake means to move with jerky motions. Babies **shake** their rattles to hear the noise and to see the movement of the rattle.

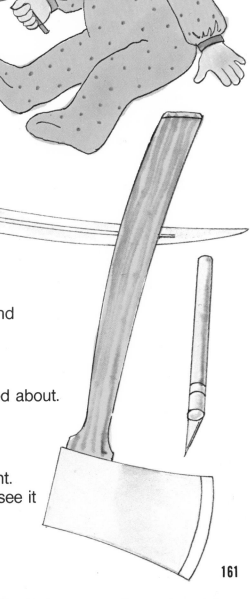

shake

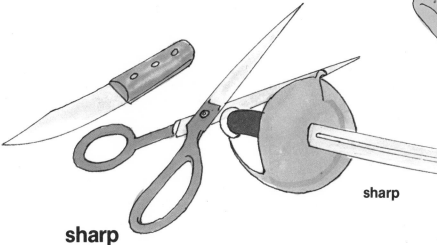

sharp

sharp

Sharp means having a thin cutting edge. Knives and scissors are **sharp**.

she

She refers to the female person who is being talked about. There's Mary. **She** is a very busy girl.

shine

Shine means giving off brightness or reflecting light.

1. The sun always **shines** but sometimes we can't see it because of the clouds overhead.

2. If you polish your shoes, they will **shine**.

Ss

shoot

When rockets are launched, they **shoot** up into the air. They are powered by a special fuel that makes them move very fast.

short

1. During the summer, some kids wear **short** pants. They are called **shorts**.

2. Vacation time always seems too **short**.

shout

Shout is a loud noise made by a person. We are told not to **shout** in the hallway at school. We can talk softly.

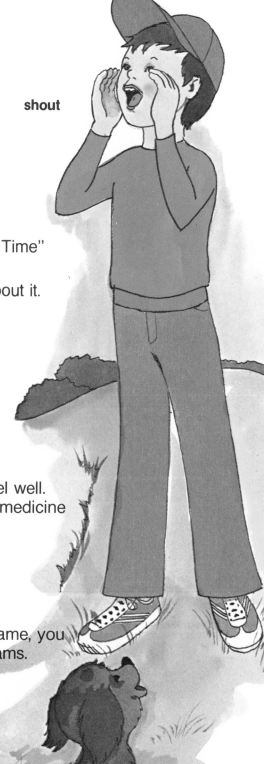

shout

show

1. I had to build a solar house for "**Show** and Tell Time" at school.

I **showed** the house and told everything I knew about it.

2. The programs on television, on radio or in the theater are called **shows.**

shut

Shut means to close.

"**Shut** the door when you come in."

sick

When you have a cold you are **sick**. You don't feel well. Sometimes you have to go to the doctor or take medicine when you are **sick**.

side

1. Boxes have six **sides**. Count the sides of your cereal box.

2. Sometimes when you are planning to play a game, you choose **sides**. All the kids are divided into two teams.

sing

Singing is a way of making music with the voice. Songs are words put to music that are **sung** by a **singer**.

sister

A **sister** is a girl child in a family with more than one child. I have two **sisters** but no brothers.

singers

sit

Sit means to rest on a chair or seat.

At school, all the kids **sit** on chairs at desks.

skate

A **skate** is a kind of shoe or attachment for a shoe that has blades or wheels on the bottom. Ice **skates** have blades so the **skater** can move smoothly over ice. Roller **skates** have wheels so the **skater** can move smoothly over the sidewalk.

sky

The **sky** is all the space that is around the earth. Airplanes fly in the **sky.** Sometimes the **sky** looks blue. Sometimes it looks grey and cloudy.

skaters

sled

A **sled** is a kind of cart that has metal blades so that it can move on ice or snow.

sleep

When people are tired they need to **sleep**. They go to bed and close their eyes, and rest quietly for several hours.

slide

Slide means to move along a slippery surface.

1. Skaters **slide** along the ice on their ice skates.

2. Baseball players **slide** along the ground to reach the bases.

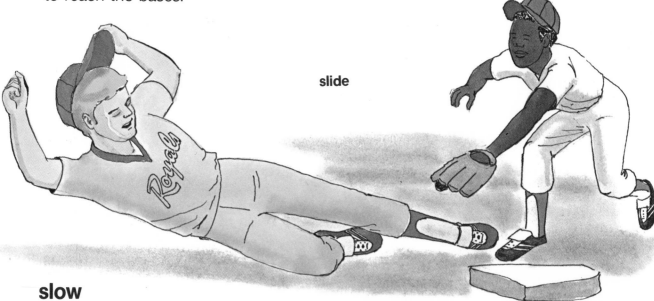

slide

slow

Slow means not fast or speedy. Turtles move along very **slowly**.

small

Small means little in size. Kids in the first grade are **small**. Kids in the sixth grade are bigger.

smell

Flowers have a sweet **smell**; skunks **smell** bad. The nose has nerves in it so that we can tell the difference between **smells.**

smile

People **smile** when they are happy. Their mouths curl upward in the corners and sometimes teeth show.

smile

smoke

Smoke is made up of very tiny pieces of material that go into the air when something is burned. **Smoke** is like a cloud and may be black, grey or any other color depending on what is burned.

snack

A **snack** is a small amount of food usually eaten between meals.

slow

sniff

Sniff means to breathe in through the nose. Rabbits wiggle their noses and seem to **sniff** the smell of things around them.

snow

Snow is water vapor that falls from clouds to earth in the form of white flakes. It **snows** in the winter in cold climates.

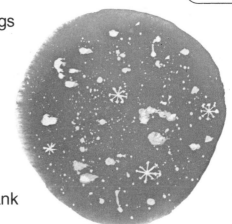

snow

some

1. "Would you like **some** cookies?" "Yes," he said, "thank you. I'll have two."

2. "Do you have any money?" "Yes, I have **some**."

south

South is a direction. If you face the sun as it sets, **south** is toward the left.

N

W   E

S

south

spell

1. To **spell** means to put letters together in the right order to form a word.

2. In stories, a **spell** is a kind of magic. Witches put **spells** on things to turn them into other things.

spill

If you knock the glass of milk over, it will **spill** all over the table.

spin

Spin means to turn round and round very fast. Tops **spin**, tires **spin**, sometimes clouds seem to **spin** around in the sky.

spin

splash

When little children jump into puddles, they **splash** water all over themselves.

spot

1. A **spot** is a mark or patch of color that is different from the color around it. If you dropped chocolate on the dress, there would be a brown **spot**.

2. A **spot** is a special place. This is the **spot** where I dropped my wallet.

Spring

Spring is one of the four seasons of the year. **Spring** comes between Winter and Summer. Flowers start to bloom in the **Spring**.

stair

A **stair** is a group of steps that rise one after the other to make it possible to go from a lower place in a building to a higher place.

splash

stamp

1. **Stamp** means to press the foot downward. He threw the match onto the ground and then **stamped** on it to be sure it was out.

2. A **stamp** is a small piece of paper with a picture on it. **Stamps** are purchased at the post office to pay the cost of mailing a letter. **Stamps** are put on letters before they are put into the mail box.

stand

When you get out of bed in the morning, you **stand** on your feet. Only your feet touch the floor. The rest of you is upright and balanced on your legs and feet. If there are no seats, you may have to **stand** on the bus.

start

Start means to begin. We will **start** to play ball right after school is over. We will finish playing at five o'clock.

stair

stay

Stay means to not go. Will you **stay** at my house until dinnertime? I would like you to **stay** here until then.

step

When you lift your foot and place it down in a new position, you have taken a **step**. Walking, dancing and marching all require different kinds of **steps**.

stitch

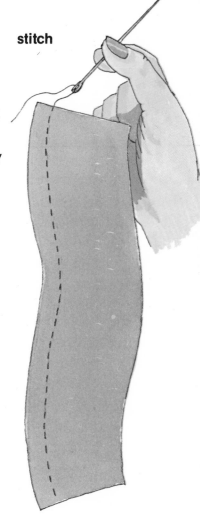

still

1. When you go to the barber to have your hair cut, you have to sit **still**. If you bounce around, the barber can't cut your hair properly.

2. The boys were here all day and they are **still** here. They haven't gone home yet.

stitch

In sewing, when you pass the needle and thread through the cloth so that it holds the cloth together, that is called a **stitch.**

stop

It snowed all night. By morning, the snow will **stop**. It will not snow any more.

story

A **story** is a way of telling about people or things. A **story** may be either written or spoken, and it may be true or imagined.

string

A **string** is a thin cord or thread. **String** is used to tie things together. Birthday presents are sometimes tied with colored **string.**

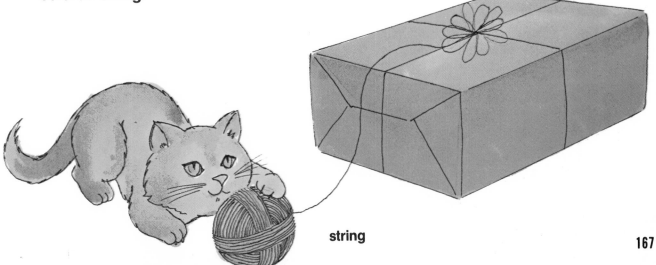

string

Summer

Summer is one of the four seasons. **Summer** comes after Spring and before Autumn. Often people take vacations in the **Summer**.

Sunday

Sunday is the first day of the week. **Sunday** is between Saturday and Monday.

swallow

When you **swallow**, food or liquid moves from your mouth down into your stomach.

sweep

I had to get the broom and **sweep** the crumbs off the floor. I moved the broom back and forth until all the crumbs were in the dustpan.

swim

Swim means to move through the water by moving the hands, feet or fins.

swing

1. In baseball, batters **swing** their bats to hit the ball when it is pitched to them.

2. Swings are seats hung on chains or ropes from a bar, or a tree branch. Children sit on the seat and move back and forth through the air on the **swing.**

swing

Can you name the things on this page that begin with the letter T? See answers at bottom of page.

ABCDEFGHIJKLMN
OPQRSTUVWXYZ

tail

A **tail** is part of the body on some animals. Squirrels have long bushy **tails**.

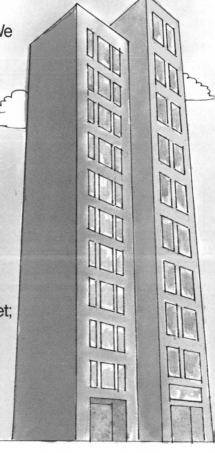

tail

take

1. Please **take** the apples over to the baby.

2. It **takes** me one hour a day to do my homework.

3. We are going to **take** part in the holiday parade.

4. My party will **take** place on Tuesday afternoon.

talk

Talk means to speak. My friend and I **talk** all day long. We have lots to say to each other.

tall

Tall means high from the ground.

1. There are many **tall** buildings in New York City.

2. I am **taller** than my brother. I am five feet **tall**.

tame

Animals that are used to being near people are **tame** animals. They are not wild.

taste

A **taste** is a particular flavor. Candy and sugar **taste** sweet; lemons **taste** sour.

tell

1. Will you **tell** me the story of Snow White? I've heard it once before.

2. Can you **tell** which of the two apples is bigger?

tall buildings

thank

When someone does something nice for you, it is right that you **thank** them.

You can say, "**Thank** you, very much."

thermometer

A **thermometer** is something used to measure heat and cold. When you have a fever, your parents will use a **thermometer** to take your temperature.

thing

A **thing** is some object, animal, or event that is not named. For example, "**Things** are going to be great today." Or, "That puppy is a pretty little **thing**."

think

1. Sometimes you have to **think** very hard to find the answer to a puzzle.

2. I don't **think** it is a good idea for us to go swimming today. It is too cold.

thread

A **thread** is a very thin cord used for sewing. **Threads** are made of twisted pieces of cotton, silk or wool.

threw

Threw is part of the verb **throw**.

He **threw** the winning basketball into the hoop.

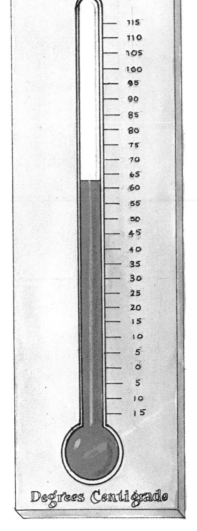

thermometer

throw

He is able to **throw** the football farther than any of the other children. When the ball goes up into the air it seems to take a long time to come down.

throw

171

thunder

Thunder is the loud noise made during a storm. **Thunder** is usually heard right after a flash of lightning.

Thursday

Thursday is the fifth day of the week. **Thursdays** come between Wednesdays and Fridays.

tired

He got up very early today and then played ball all day. He is very **tired**. He will need to go to sleep early tonight.

to

1. We go **to** school every day.

2. I like **to** sing.

too

I like ice cream. My brother also likes it. He, **too,** likes ice cream.

top

The roof is at the **top** of the house. The basement is at the bottom.

true

The sun rises in the east, and sets in the west. That is a fact; it is **true**.

top

try

1. I have butter, flour, milk, eggs and sugar. I am going to mix them all together and **try** to make a cake.

2. When we shop to buy shoes, I always have to **try** them on to see if they fit right.

Tuesday

Tuesday is the third day of the week. **Tuesdays** come between Mondays and Wednesdays.

turn

1. When you finish reading one page of your book, just **turn** the page and read the next page.

2. You can have the first **turn** in the game; then it will be my **turn** to play.

The girl is **trying** on shoes.

Can you name the things on this page that begin with the letters U or V? See answers at bottom of page.

ABCDEFGHIJKLMNOPQRST**UV**WXYZ

ugly

Some medicine has a bitter taste. It is **ugly** tasting.

umbrella

An **umbrella** is a kind of screen that people carry to keep sun or rain off them. **Umbrellas** are made of cloth or paper on wood or metal frames.

umbrella

unicorn

A **unicorn** is an imaginary animal that has a body of a horse with a long horn growing out of its forehead.

up

1. Airplanes go **up** into the sky when they leave the ground.

2. My skates were lost, but they have just turned **up**.

us

They gave **us** hamburgers for lunch. We ate them quickly.

use

When I eat dinner, I **use** a knife and fork to cut the food and lift it into my mouth.

usual

I get up every day at eight o'clock. It is **usual** for me to get up at that time.

unicorn

175

vacation

1. We go to school for ten months and have two months **vacation.** We don't go to school then.

2. We go to the beach every day during **vacation**.

vaccination

When you go to the doctor, she sometimes gives you a needle in the arm that has medicine in it so you will not get some disease. That is called a **vaccination**.

valentine

A **valentine** is a message or gift that is given so another person will know that you care about them.

vanilla

Vanilla is used to give a certain taste to some foods. It is made from a bean-like fruit.

valentine

very

I'm happy most of the time, but I am **very** happy when I am with my dog.

village

A **village** is a small town in the country. There are stores and houses and a school and church in a **village**.

volcano

A **volcano** is a vent or opening in the earth's crust. Rocks, lava, gas, and steam come through the opening. As the rocks pile on top of each other they form **volcanic** cones that look like hills or mountains.

volcano

Can you name the things on this page that begin with the letter W? See answers at bottom of page.

ABCDEFGHIJKLMNOPQRSTUVWXYZ

wag

Wag means to move from side to side quickly. Puppies **wag** their tails when they are happy.

wait

We got to the airport early and had to **wait** two hours before the plane arrived.

wake

We go to sleep at night. In the morning we **wake** up, get out of bed and get dressed. When you are not asleep, you are **awake**.

walk

Walk means to move on foot one step after another. I **walk** to school. It is a long **walk**.

wall

A **wall** is the side of a building or room. There are usually four **walls** in a room.

want

I have two cookies. I don't **want** anymore. I do **want** a glass of milk though.

warm

In the winter it may be cold outside. We go inside to get **warm.** The fireplace keeps the house **warm**.

walkers

walking

wave

1. A **wave** is a moving swell or ridge on the top of the water in the ocean. As **waves** move towards the shore, they crash on the beach and then the water moves out to sea again.

2. Mom raised her hand and shook her hand back and forth. She was **waving** to me as I came down the street.

wave

wax

Wax is a thick, soft material found in certain plants and animals. Bees make **wax** and use it to build their honeycombs. **Wax** is used to make candles.

wax

way

1. There are two **ways** to go to school. My friend and I like to go the long **way**. It takes longer, but it is more fun.

2. This is the **way** grandma makes cookies. I do things differently when I make them.

we

I am going. You are going, too. **We** will go together.

weak

Weak means not strong. When I had a cold, I was too **weak** to get up from bed. I got stronger after a few days.

weather

Weather is the climate condition. **Weather** may be hot or cold, rainy or sunny. At different times of the year the **weather** is different.

weather

web

A **web** is a collection of thin threads that are put together in a special way. Spiders spin **webs**.

Wednesday

Wednesday is the fourth day of the week. **Wednesday** comes after Tuesday and before Thursday.

weigh

We use scales to find out how much a thing **weighs**. The **weight** of anything is its amount of heaviness.

well

1. I am not sick anymore. I am **well** now.

2. A **well** is a place deep in the ground. **Wells** are dug to get water, oil and gas from them.

were

Were is part of the verb **be**.

Were you going to play ball today? I will **be** able to play, if you can.

west

West is a direction.
The sun sets in the **West**.

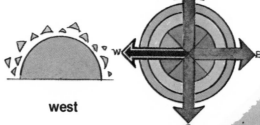

west

whale

A **whale** is a very large animal that lives in the ocean. **Whales** look like fish but are not fish. They are mammals.

whale

wharf

A **wharf** is a building or buildings built along the shore so that ships can tie up next to them to load and unload the things they carry.

what

1. What do you want to eat for breakfast? Do you want eggs or cereal?

2. What day do you want to go marketing?

wheel

wheat

wheat

Wheat is a plant. The grain from **wheat** can be ground into flour for making bread and other foods.

wheel

Wheels are round objects that make it possible to move heavy things along flat surfaces. Bicycles, automobiles, and many other vehicles have **wheels** with tires. Skateboards and roller skates have **wheels.**

where

I brought your bicycle back to you. **Where** shall I put it? Shall I leave it indoors or outdoors?

whether

I would like to know **whether** you can come to my party or not. If you can't, I'll be sad.

which

1. You can have this one or that one. **Which** do you want?

2. The horse on **which** I rode was very gentle.

while

A **while** is an amount of time.

1. I want to see her **while** she is here.

2. I met your brother a long **while** ago.

whisker

1. A **whisker** is a hair that grows on the side of a man's face.

2. Whiskers are long bristly hairs that grow around the mouths of some animals.

whisper

Whisper means to speak in soft and low tones.

who

1. Someone came in. **Who** was it?

2. The girl **who** sings so nicely was in to see us today.

whole

Whole means the entire thing. My friend and I ate the **whole** watermelon.

why

Why did you do that? What is the reason you did that?

whiskers

wide

1. There is a big space to cross between this side of the street and that side. It is a **wide** street.

2. The **width** of the street is about a hundred feet.

wife

A **wife** is a woman who is married. She is her husband's **wife**.

wild

Animals that have not grown up around people are called **wild** animals. Wolves are **wild** animals. Cats and dogs are not **wild** animals.

will

Tomorrow is a school day. We **will** go to school.

win

My school tennis team played against another team. We tried hard to **win** but lost anyway. The other team **won**.

wind

1. Wind is moving air or air current. In a tornado or gale the **wind** moves very fast and may cause damage.

2. Wind means to bend or turn about. Did you remember to **wind** the clock today?

(This word is pronounced differently for each meaning. Please ask your teacher or your parents how these words sound.)

windmill

A **windmill** is a machine used for grinding or pumping. **Windmills** use the power of the wind to move long, flat pieces of wood or metal. As the blades move they produce power.

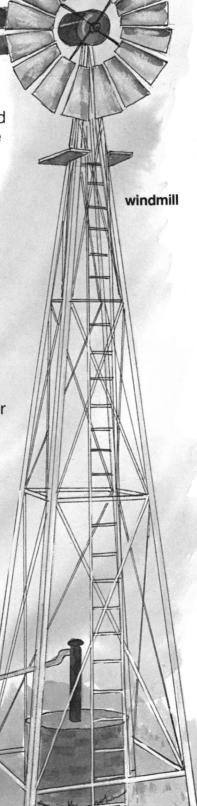

windmill

window

A **window** is an opening in the wall of a building. **Windows** are made of glass so they let the sunlight in.

wing

1. Wings are the parts of the bodies of insects or birds that make it possible for them to fly.

2. Airplanes have **wings** so the air can move over them in a certain way and the plane can lift off the ground.

wings

wink

Wink means to open and close one eyelid very quickly, as a kind of signal.

winter

Winter

Winter is one of the four seasons of the year. **Winter** is the cold season of the year. **Winter** comes between Autumn and Spring.

wipe

Wipe means to rub lightly with a cloth, towel or hand.

wire

A **wire** is a very thin piece of metal. **Wire** can be bent easily. Electricity travels through **wires**.

wish

On your birthday when you blow out the candles on your cake you close your eyes and hope for something you want. That is a **wish**.

witch

In legends and stories, a **witch** is a woman who has special magical powers.

with

I will go **with** you. We will go together.

wizard

A **wizard** is a person who can do magic. **Wizards,** in stories, can make things disappear.

woke

Woke is part of the verb **wake.**

Today I **woke** up early. Tomorrow I will **wake** up early, too.

witch

wolf

A **wolf** is a wild animal belonging to the dog family. **Wolves** look something like dogs but are very fast and very dangerous. They live in forest land.

woman

A **woman** is a grownup female person. Girls become **women** when they grow up.

won

Won is part of the verb **win.**

I **won** a medal for spelling last year. I don't know if I will **win** again this year.

wizard

wonder

1. I don't know who will be in the game today. I think our team might win. I **wonder** if I am right.

2. I was thinking about the team that is playing today. I **wondered** about them. I **wondered** which team has the best players.

wonderful

It is **wonderful** to be able to read and write. It makes you feel good to be able to learn by reading and writing.

wood

The trees and branches of trees are made of **wood. Wood** is used for building, for making furniture, and for many other things. When **wood** is burned it gives off heat.

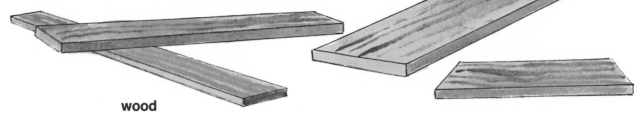

wood

wool

Wool is fine, soft curly hair from sheep and certain other animals. **Wool** is used to make cloth for clothing and for other purposes.

word

A **word** is a sound or group of sounds that can be spoken or written and understood.

wore

Wore is part of the verb **wear.**

She **wore** her yellow dress yesterday. Tomorrow she will **wear** a red dress.

wool

work

1. When I come home from school, I have chores to do. I **work** for an hour, walking the dog and feeding my pets and cleaning my room.

2. My dad **works** as a writer and mom **works** as a teacher.

3. I tried to get my sister to take us to the movies, but my plan didn't **work**. She wouldn't take us.

worker

A **worker** is a person who **works.** Most **workers** work to earn money. People **work** at jobs.

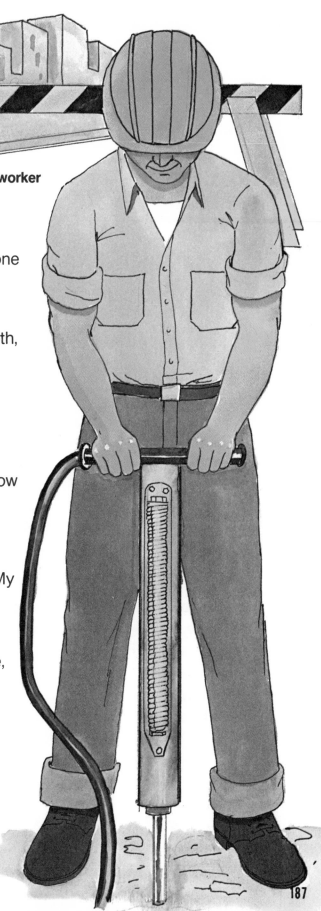

worker

world

The **world** is the planet Earth and everyone and everything on it.

worm

Worms are small animals that have smooth, long, round bodies without arms or legs. **Worms** move by creeping and crawling. Some **worms** live in the earth.

worn

These are my favorite shoes, but I have been **wearing** them too long. They are now **worn** out. They are torn and shabby.

worry

Worry means to think about things that make us feel uneasy or uncomfortable. My dog is sick. I am **worried** about him.

worse

Last night I had a fever. Today it is **worse**, and so I can not go to school. My temperature has gone up.

worst

This is the **worst** ice cream soda I've ever had. Every other soda I've had has been better.

would

Your birthday **will** be in two weeks. **Would** you like to have a party? I think I **would** like a party this year.

wrap
Wrap means to put something around something else. Gifts are usually wrapped with pretty paper.

wrapping

wrinkle
A **wrinkle** is a small crease or fold. When you frown or squint you get **wrinkles** around your eyes and forehead.

Aa Bb Cc Dd Ee Ff Gg Hh Ii Jj Kk Ll
Oo Pp Qq Rr Ss Tt Uu Vv Ww Xx Yy Z

writing

write
1. One of the first things children learn in school is how to **write** the alphabet. They use paper and pencil and learn how to make letters and then to form words.

2. When you think up a story and **write** it down for people to read, you are a **writer**.

written
Written is part of the verb **write**.

A story was **written** by my sister. She **wrote** it when she was eight years old.

wrong
Wrong means not correct.

1. This is the **wrong** shoe size. It does not fit me.

2. It is **wrong** to hit other children. People should not hit other people.

wrote
Wrote is part of the verb **write**.

She **wrote** the story at school. Tonight she will **write** another story.

Can you name the things on this page that begin with the letters X, Y or Z? See answers at bottom of page.

ABCDEFGHIJKLMN
OPQRSTUVWXYZ

x-rays

X-rays are rays of energy that can pass through solid objects. **X-rays** help doctors photograph the inside of a patient's body and to discover if they are ill.

xylophone

A **xylophone** is a musical instrument that is made up of a series of wooden or metal bars that are sounded by striking with a small wooden hammer.

xylophone

yard

The **yard** is the ground around the house or other buildings. I have swings and other toys in my **yard**.

yawn

When you are tired or drowsy sometimes you open your mouth wide and draw in air as a deep breath. That is called a **yawn**.

yell

Yell means to cry out with a loud, strong, clear sound. My little brother **yelled** when he thought he was lost.

yes

Yes is the oppostie of **no**. "Do you want some milk?" I said. "**Yes**, thank you," Denise said. I poured two glasses of milk for us and we drank them.